I0038967

The New Constitution for Modern America

Based on Justice and Individual Rights

by

Alex Hussein Ahmedinejahd

Copyright

The New Constitution for Modern America. Copyright © 2013 by Alex Hussein Ahmedinejahd

All rights reserved. Published and printed in the United States of America. No part of this book may be used, transmitted, stored or reproduced in any manner whatsoever without prior permission except in the case of brief quotations embodied in critical articles and reviews.

Request for permission should be addressed to: Alex Hussein Ahmedinejahd via email at AlexAhmedinejahd@yahoo.com.

First Published 2013 by Alex Hussein Ahmedinejahd

Table of Contents

which, is, The Constitution and all laws which...
obeyed, and all governmental laws...

Introduction

How does anyone re-write one of the most iconic documents in human history without seeming to be cocky and self-righteous? It is without doubt an incredibly daunting task. However, if one takes it as an academic project and look to modernize a document that was written over some 225 years ago, it isn't as daunting nor overwhelming as it may seem. Regardless, and admittedly, it is still a difficult undertaking. However, there is no doubt that the current Constitution is in need of modern updates and certain principles need to be clarified and codified that have been left vague – perhaps deliberately – that is the crux of many unnecessary and controversial strife in our country.

Also, the concept of a republic is no longer necessary and states are an obsolete concept in our country. This is because the reason for states is no longer valid. When the country was founded, smaller states were concerned about being dominated by larger states and southern states were concerned that the northern states would force the southern states to abolish slavery, among other issues. Therefore, the divisions that drove the new country to form a republic, have senators and give states extraordinary powers are no longer issues that are relevant to our country in the 21st century.

Finally, and most importantly, we have to consider the influence of religion over politics and our political system. There are too many issues that are driven by religious doctrine in our society, which, by definition, strives to marginalize the minority and seeks to force the will of the religious majority on all. This is very wrong and should not be allowed. For example, many oaths and even the pledge of allegiance seek to force religious doctrine and obedience on all. Let's take the pledge of allegiance as an example. It reads as follows: I pledge allegiance to the flag of the United States of America, and to the republic, for which it stands, one nation, *under god*, indivisible, with liberty and justice for all. So, does this mean that if an individual does not believe in god – any god – that they cannot pledge allegiance to the USA? What if an individual, who doesn't believe in god takes the pledge of allegiance? Does this mean that the individual is a hypocrite for taking the pledge of allegiance? This is quite obviously not right nor fair. Therefore, to make the pledge of allegiance fair to all and applicable to all in our country, it should read as follows: I pledge allegiance to the United States of America, for which it stands, one nation, under the Constitution with liberty and justice for all. There are numerous other examples of religious doctrine attempting to dictate to all what is right and wrong and moral and immoral. However, it should not be difficult to understand that it is wrong to force one's philosophical thinking on everyone. Yet people continue to do so on the scant evidence that it is god's will, whichever god that may be. This is outrageous.

More to the point, the forced adoption of religious doctrine is very un-American and, therefore, influences of religious doctrine must be completely eradicated from politics, law and governance. This is not to say that each of us does not have the right to our own beliefs; we absolutely do, but we do not have the right to force our beliefs on others. Also, forcing religious doctrine on people who don't believe in religion implies that religious doctrine is the only truth and only moral philosophy that should be respected and obeyed, and this is simply not true.

First, people who don't believe in a religion can be as moral, if not more moral than religious people, and their beliefs just as valid, if not more. Second, being an American is unlike any other citizen of any other country or empire that exists or existed in human history. It is exceptionally different and, most importantly, the most moral of all human existence. Specifically, being an American, unlike any other country, is not about one's religious beliefs or about skin color, ancestry, creed, race, gender, sexual orientation, or any visible outward signs of segregation.

For us, it is about our philosophy, but not about religious philosophy. Our philosophy, like our citizenship is unique in human history. For the first time in human existence, we believe in the equality of people and inalienable rights accorded to those people; rights that were not widely available to any other citizens of any other country in the world, past or present. These inalienable rights would include, but are not limited to, the right to free speech, freedom of religion, freedom of the press, assembly, have redress of grievances from our government, bear arms, vote for our government, change our government peaceably, representation, public jury trials, due process, face accusers, appropriate punishment for crime, not testify against oneself, compensation for loss of private property, the separation of power, and one's assets and possessions, i.e., no illegal search and seizures. Individually, these rights are highly unique in many respects to our country, Americans and very special to our existence; however, taken together, these rights accorded to any individual are unheard of in human history.

These inalienable rights, combined with the capitalist ideals are what make America, America. Therefore, the belief and practice of these rights and economic model is what makes an American, an American. In short, we are the only country in the world where the right to citizenship is defined by our philosophical beliefs (but not religious beliefs) and identity. This is unlike any other country in the world, past or present.

This concept of America – what I refer to as Americanism – is and must be embodied by the Constitution. However, as stated previously, the Constitution, as great as it is, it is somewhat out of touch with today's reality and many aspects of the current Constitution is too vague for modern society. In particular, the first Amendment to the Constitution regarding religion is too vague. It states that, "Congress shall make no laws respecting an establishment of religion." What it should state is that, "No laws, regulations, rules, legislation, policy and the like will be created with regard to or in consideration of any religious or philosophical doctrine." In addition, the Constitution should have read that, "No one group or their doctrine shall be favored over another and cause prejudice or segregation in our society," or something there to. Next, the Constitution should make it perfectly clear that individual rights must prevail over societal rights in every respect and that the government shall not act as a function of force in our society in any manner. Lastly, the Constitution should have made it very clear that taking assets and wealth from one group by force to support another is not only immoral, but also catastrophic for the long-term health of our country. Therefore, the Constitution should have specified only a handful of items that the Federal government should be allowed to fund, and the Constitution should have clearly forbidden the redistribution of wealth, which is theft and tantamount to putting shackles on the rich and calling it jewelry.

It is with these particular short-comings of the Constitution in mind that I have set out to rewrite the holiest of documents to the American people. This is not to say that the Constitution, as written, should not be marveled at and read with awe; it should be for it is the first of its kind and tantamount to inventing some genius revolutionary product that transforms the world for the better for eternity. However, like all new revolutionary product, an update of the product is warranted and necessary as our understanding of the product improves, and we outgrow the novelty of the item. Therefore, as great as the Constitution was when it was first written, as we understand the document better, as we grow with the use of the document, and as we discover some of the deficiencies of the document and know the implications and consequences of those deficiencies, it would be to our betterment to rewrite the Constitution for modern times. And, as cocky and distasteful as the idea of rewriting the Constitution may seem to some, nevertheless, it is without doubt long overdue.

I would appreciate any constructive comments and feedback on my rewrite of the Constitution. This feedback can be left on my website, www.UndertheConstitutionwithLibertyandJusticeforAll.com or via email at alexahmedinejahd@yahoo.com. Thank you for buying and reading this book.

If you enjoyed this book, please read, "Under the Constitution with Liberty and Justice for all," available at www.CreateSpace.com/3978962. It is a companion to this book and would explain a lot of the issues and thoughts behind why I chose to rewrite the Constitution the way I did.

The New Constitution for Modern America

The name of the country shall be changed from The United States of America to The Constitutional Democracy of America (CDA), as the concept of a republic is no longer valid to our country.

The principle foundation of the Constitutional Democracy of America (CDA)

We the people of the Constitutional Democracy of America (CDA), in order to form a more perfect democratic country, establish *Justice*, insure domestic tranquility, unity, provide for the common defense, infrastructure and education of the country, promote the general and overall welfare equally and Justly, and secure the blessings of life, liberty and pursuit of happiness to ourselves and our posterity, do ordain and establish this Constitution for the Constitutional Democracy of America (CDA).

Basis of the Constitution for the Constitutional Democracy of America (CDA)

Section 1. The CDA will not discriminate against its Citizens and Permanent Residents and the Constitution shall apply equally and Justly to all Citizens and Permanent Residents.

We hold these truths to be self-evident that all people that are citizens (Citizens; defined below; unless otherwise specifically excluded or exempted) or legal permanent residents (Permanent Residents; defined below; unless otherwise specifically excluded or exempted) of the Constitutional Democracy of America (CDA) are entitled to the same rights and liberties guaranteed by the Constitution of the Constitutional Democracy of America, herein scripted, regardless of race, gender, sexual orientation, skin-color, race, ancestry, creed, philosophical (including religious) beliefs, intelligence (unless otherwise specifically excluded or exempted), income, wealth, occupation, physical or mental (unless otherwise specifically excluded or exempted) handicaps or illnesses, educational accomplishments, political affiliation, location of residence, or any other criteria or measure that can separate, segregate, categorize or divide Citizens and Permanent Residents (together the People of the CDA or People, Peoples, Person or Persons) of the CDA.

Section 2. All laws shall be moral and Just.

All laws, legislations, rules, regulations, edicts and alike must be proven to be moral and Just, and consistently, fairly and equally applied to all People of the CDA. Also, any violation, abridging, encroachment, limiting, curbing, suspending, curtailing, revoking or the like of any of the People's Inalienable Rights, which are outlined in Article II, is forever illegal and immoral and shall not be condoned in any way, shape or form whether or not a specific law exists to cover such transgressions other than a declaration of Martial Law under only very specific instances as outlined in this Constitution.

Section 3. All laws must be applied equally, but the premise of all laws must be Justice not equality.

The basis of our Judicial system must embody the moral edict that *equality isn't always Just, but Justice applied equally is always fair*. Accordingly, all laws, legislation, rules, regulations, judicial pronouncements, edicts and the like, and all business and all personal interactions, conduct, responsibilities, duties, obligations, behaviors, practices, and the like must be conducted with Justice as the only operating principle. All laws, regulations, rules, rights, edicts and the like must be equally applied to all People in every way. By definition, this section does not allow for the existence of a so called "progressive" tax system or for any quotas of any kind.

Section 4. Amendments to the Constitution shall be initiated by the President, ratified by Congress and approved by the Supreme Court.

All amendments to the Constitution shall originate from the President, and must be ratified by a minimum of three-quarters of the Members of Congress. Once ratified by Congress, a minimum of two-thirds of the Justices of the Supreme Court must agree to the constitutionality of the proposed and ratified amendment. If the Supreme Court does not approve the proposed and ratified amendment, but the President and the leadership of Congress wish to pursue its approval by the Supreme Court then Congress shall reconsider the amendment, modify it, ratify it with three-quarters of Congress voting in favor of the modified amendment, and, if the President agrees with the modifications made by Congress, present the modified Amendment for approval to the Supreme Court. If rejected by the Supreme Court a second time, but the President and the leadership of Congress wish to continue pursuing the approval of the modified Amendment then Congress shall reconsider the modified amendment, make any modifications deemed necessary, submit it for ratification by at least 90% of Congress, secure the approval of the President then seek a country-wide referendum. For the modified amendment to become part of the Constitution, a minimum of 90% of the Citizens of the CDA must vote to approve the proposed, modified and ratified amendment. If 90% of the Citizens vote to approve the proposed, modified and ratified amendment then the proposed, modified and ratified amendment will be recorded into the Constitution and be accorded equal status and treatment as all other Articles and Sections of the Constitution.

Section 5. Pledge of Allegiance

The Pledge of Allegiance shall be read as follows: I pledge allegiance to the Constitutional Democracy of America for which it stands, one-nation, under the Constitution with Liberty and Justice for all.

This pledge of allegiance shall be taken by every Citizen and Permanent Resident of the CDA and will not be subject to change under any circumstances and will not be allowed to be amended under any circumstances, including amendment by the Congress of the CDA.

Section 6. Adulthood and Age of Consent and Age of Self-Selection

For purposes of criminal prosecution, sexual consent, self-determination and, in general, division between adulthood and childhood, unless Congress otherwise legislates, the age of adulthood shall be deemed to start at 18 years of age. In case of criminal prosecution, the presiding judge will determine whether an alleged perpetrator shall be tried as an adult or as a child.

However, for the purpose of determining the appropriate age for drinking, gambling, drug use, or other forms of activities that may be deemed potentially perilous to one's physical or financial existence or that which is proven to be addictive or otherwise deemed a vice, the youngest aged adult permitted to self-select such activities shall be equal to that of the voting age.

Definitions

President: The President of the Constitutional Democracy of America (President or POTCDA) will be the head of the government and within the Office of the President, the executive powers of the Constitutional Democracy of America (CDA) will be enshrined. The POTCDA will be elected into office as prescribed within this document.

Vice-President: The Vice-President of the Constitutional Democracy of America (Vice-President or Vice-POTCDA) will be the Leader of Congress. In addition, the Vice POTCDA will assume the responsibilities, duties and powers as well as receive all of the privileges, benefits and honor accorded to the POTCDA in the event that the POTCDA is incapacitated, dies in office or otherwise unable to execute the duties, responsibilities and powers of the Office of the POTCDA as prescribed within this document. The Vice-POTCDA will be elected into office as prescribed within this document.

Congress: The Congress shall be constituted as the legislative body of government of the CDA and its members shall be elected to office by direct vote as prescribed in this document from each of their respective Congressional District and shall be referred to as a Member of Congress, Members of Congress, Congressional Member, Congressional Members, Member or Members within this document. The Members of Congress shall make all Federal laws that govern all Peoples and residents – except where treaties make exceptions – of the CDA and residents of territories under the jurisdiction of the CDA. Congress shall be composed of only one chamber. The number of Congressional Members shall be determined according to the prescription outlined within this document. Congress will be the only body authorized to impeach select officials as prescribed herein. Congress must ratify all treaties, and ratify all amendments to the Constitution, and approve all nominations made by the President as outlined in this document. Congress shall have the sole power to create legislation to enforce all provisions of the Constitution of the CDA.

Supreme Court: The Supreme Court of the CDA shall embody the final judicial authority in the CDA and shall deal with all disputes and controversies domestic and foreign that involves the People and residents of the CDA, the Federal government, or interpretation of the Constitution and Federal legislations. The Chief Justice of the Supreme Court will be the presiding Judge in any impeachment proceedings involving the impeachment of members of the Executive or Legislative Branch that were elected as outlined herein. Members of the Supreme Court will be selected according to the procedures specified within this document. The Supreme Court will be comprised of nine members.

Citizen of the Constitutional Democracy of America: A Citizen of the CDA is defined as one who has all of the rights, privileges and protections afforded under the Constitution. Any persons that are legal Citizens of the United States of America (USA) at the time of ratification of this Constitution will be automatically Citizens of the CDA. Any persons that are legal permanent residents of the United States of America at the time of ratification of this Constitution will be automatically Permanent Residents of the CDA. No change in status will be accorded to any legal or illegal foreigners residing in the USA at the time of ratification of this Constitution.

Citizenship and path to Citizenship: Any persons born to a Citizen of the CDA will be a Citizen of the CDA and will have the full rights, privileges and protection accorded by this document as a Citizen of the CDA, regardless of where the person was born. Anyone born in the territorial boundaries of the CDA or jurisdictions subject to CDA's Constitution, rules, regulations, laws, legislations and the like and where at least one parent is a Permanent Resident shall be a Citizen of the CDA. Anyone born outside of the territorial boundaries or jurisdiction of the CDA to at least one parent that is a Permanent Resident shall be accorded the status of a Permanent Resident of the CDA. The difference between Citizen and Permanent Resident will be two-fold: 1) The Citizen will be allowed to vote in any and all government elections, while the Permanent Resident will not be allowed to vote in any government elections; and 2) the Permanent Resident will be required to pay an additional 10% in income taxes so long as they choose to remain a Permanent Resident past the 3rd year of Permanent Residency. Anyone born in the territories of the CDA or born to a parent of a citizen of a territory of the CDA shall remain a citizen of that territory, but not a Citizen or Permanent Resident of the CDA.

Permanent Resident: Permanent Residents will be legal immigrants to the CDA. Permanent Residents will be allowed to stay Permanent Residents; however, if after three (3) years, the Permanent Resident fails to attain their Citizenship in the CDA, the Permanent Resident will be subject to an additional income tax of 10% above and beyond what Citizens who make the same income would pay. Congress will set rules, regulations, and quotas for governing immigration to the CDA.

Skilled Labor Permanent Resident: Qualified foreigners that graduate from CDA institutions with majors or skills that are deemed to be in short supply by industries in the CDA, and attain legal employment within 6 months of graduation will be automatically given full Permanent Resident status upon their first day of employment. If the individual is married or engaged then the spouse or fiancée will also receive full Permanent Resident status at the same time as the qualified foreigner. If the individual has children then the children will also receive full Permanent Resident status at the same time as the qualified foreigner, assuming the qualified foreigner has full custody of the children. To qualify for the automatic Permanent Residency, the foreigner, spouse or fiancée, and children must not have a criminal record in their home country or in the CDA, is not a fugitive from either government, is not associated with terrorist groups, and the foreigner must have legal full-time employment within 6 months of graduation.

Investor Permanent Resident: Qualified foreigners that invest twenty-times or more of the average income of a Citizen over the last measurable five years into the CDA economy – including securities markets -- or directly create two (2) or more jobs in the CDA will be given the option of becoming a full Permanent Resident of the CDA. If the individual is married or engaged then the spouse or fiancée will also have the option of receiving full Permanent Resident status at the same time as the qualified foreign investor. If the individual has children then the children will also have the option to receive full Permanent Resident status at the same time as the qualified foreign investor, assuming the qualified foreign investor has full custody of the children. To qualify for the automatic Permanent Residency, the foreign investor, spouse or fiancée, and children must not have a criminal record in their home country or in the CDA, is not a fugitive from either government, is not associated with terrorist groups, and the foreign investor must meet the investment conditions as outlined above.

Qualified Spouse: For the purpose of immigration into the CDA, a spouse will be defined as a single individual, regardless of gender, whom the individual is legally married to. If an individual is married to more than one person then the individual must designate a single person as their legal spouse when immigrating to the CDA. All other persons that the individual was married to in their home country will be considered ex-spouses under CDA law.

Illegal and Temporary Resident: Any persons born to legal foreign residents of the CDA will be given the option of becoming Citizens of the CDA at age 18 with proof of birth within the territorial boundaries of the CDA. Any persons born to illegal residents of the CDA will be given the option of becoming a temporary resident (Temporary Resident) of the CDA upon turning 18 years old with proof of birth in the CDA and proof of ability to earn their own living within the territorial boundaries of the CDA or attend an institution of higher learning such as a federally certified college or university, or federally supported college or university.

Also, while a Temporary Resident of the CDA, the individual will be subject to 125% of income taxes levied and due from individuals that are Citizens and earn the same income, but will not qualify for any benefits and privileges accorded to the People of the CDA other than items absolutely necessary to make a living such as a driver's license, providing the Temporary Resident passes all tests and meets all other requirements to earn the necessary privilege.

While a Temporary Resident of the CDA, the individual shall not be permitted to petition the government for legal immigration of any of the person's relatives. The state of temporary residency will last 18 years, but may be reduced by one year for every year the Temporary Resident pays double the normal income taxes otherwise due from a Citizen that makes the same income, or by the same number of months that the Temporary Resident resided in their home country before turning 18 and after being born. However, regardless of any previous provisions, the Temporary Resident status will not be shortened by more than 13 years.

Any children (under 18 years of age) of illegal immigrants born in this country must remain with the parent(s) under all situations and circumstances. If one parent is deported, but somehow the other is not, the children must remain with the mother.

Once the prescribed temporary residency period is over, the Temporary Resident must take both an oral and written test of the English language, a knowledge test of USA and CDA history, and a test of the Constitution of the CDA and pass each with a minimum score of 85% out of 100% in order to earn their Permanent Resident status, at which point all rights, and privileges accorded to Permanent Residents will be accorded to the former Temporary Resident. Any Temporary Resident that does not pass all three tests within 3 attempts per test will be deported. Tests are to be conducted once every three months at primary or secondary schools in each municipality as necessary and all tests shall have a combination of multiple choice and short written answers and essays. Once the Temporary Residency period is over, the Temporary Resident must pass the test for Permanent Resident within three (3) years or be deported.

All other illegal residents in the CDA will be deported, unless they meet all of the following conditions: 1) they have a legal place of residence, 2) The illegal resident has a full-time job, which they've held for more than one year, 3) the illegal immigrant pays double the income tax normally collected from Citizens of the CDA that earn the same income, which shall be collected from their pay directly on a periodic basis that coincides with their pay period, 4) have a bank account where their pay is directly deposited and allows for the IRS to withdraw the taxes due immediately, 5) have not broken any laws, rules, legislations, regulations and the like, 6) saves 10% of their earnings in a special bank account that does not allow for withdrawals – this money is to be used for emergencies only overseen by a parole officer of the Immigration and Naturalization Services or its successor and assigns, and 7) the illegal immigrant must report to an assigned parole officer on a monthly basis with proof of employment, and the most recent banking statement. The illegal resident will meet with the parole office on the illegal resident's day off, which may be Saturday or Sunday. However, all parole officers shall not work for more than five (5) days per week.

If the illegal resident loses their job, they must immediately look for another job and live off of the forced savings until they find another job. If they are unable to find another job before their savings are depleted then they will be deported. If any of these conditions are violated, the illegal resident is subject to immediate deportation.

Children of illegal immigrants must remain in school and must pass each and all of their classes with at least an 85% out of 100% or they and their parents will be deported. While in school, children of illegal residents will be afforded all rights and privileges accorded to other children in the CDA.

All illegal immigrants that continue to meet the terms and conditions outlined above for five years will be given Temporary Resident status and subject to all requirements of Temporary Resident status. All other illegal residents will be deported immediately without trial, appeal or due process.

Philosophy: The definition of philosophy shall also include any and all religions.

Military: The armed forces of the CDA will be referred to as the Military in this document and shall include the Army, Navy, Air Force, Marines, and Coast Guard and may include any future Space Force as deemed necessary by the President and approved by Congress.

Article I. Balance of Power in the CDA must be maintained at all times: Presidential Power to Propose, Congressional Power to Enforce and Judicial Power to Interpret the Articles of the Constitution

Section 1. During peacetime and non-national-emergency situations

The President shall have the sole power to propose Amendments to the Constitution or rules, regulations, legislations, laws or the like to enforce any and all provisions of the Constitution. The Congress shall have the sole power to enforce, by appropriate legislation, laws, regulations, rules, and the like, any and all provisions of this Constitution. The Supreme Court shall have the sole power to rule on the Constitutionality of any rules, regulations, laws, legislations and the like perpetuated, promulgated, required, enforced or attempted to enforce or the like by any individual, government, group, businesses, charities, non-governmental organizations, not-for-profit entities, clubs, associations, institutions, organizations, and the like in the CDA or subject to the jurisdiction of the CDA.

Section 2. Martial law: The President has the right to suspend certain rights, but not without oversight

National emergencies shall be defined only as follows: 1) A physical invasion of the territorial integrity of the CDA, 2) an epidemic/pandemic of a deadly disease of national proportion, 3) a non-physical invasion of the territorial integrity of the CDA (e.g., cyber attack) that threatens to immobilize the normal functioning of the CDA, including, the economy, civilian and government institutions, or general quality of life, 4) a national armed rebellion or insurrection, or 5) an attempt to overthrow the government through non-qualified means. In such situations, the President with the support of the Vice President and the two-thirds majority of the President's Cabinet will have the right to declare martial law and suspend certain rights of the People and all residents of the CDA.

Also, when the President declares martial law, the President must also specify which potentially qualified Sections of Article II will be suspended and declare why and how the suspension of those rights will restore order to the CDA. Additionally, if the following oversights and concurrence is not forth-coming within 10 days then the declaration of martial law will be vacated: 1) This is self-evident, but it must be reported by the general and broad media and Congress must declare that the CDA is in a state of war by majority vote; 2) This should also be self-evident, but it must be reported by the general and broad media, and Congress must concur that a deadly epidemic/pandemic of national proportion exists by majority vote, 3) the intelligence community supported by civilian experts not associated with the government must concur with the President and must publicly testify to such an event in front of Congress and the

President must show that without the suspension of certain rights that order and return to normalcy cannot be restored and Congress must concur by majority vote, 4) this should be self-evident, but it must be reported by the general and broad media, Congress must concur by majority vote and the rebellion or insurrection must involve more than 10% of the People of the CDA, and 5) the President must publicly expose the suspected conspirators, and Congress must concur by majority vote. In all cases, the Supreme Court must support the President's decision to declare martial law within 30 days by at least a two-thirds majority.

Also, Congressional concurrence for the declaration of martial law by the President must be obtained through two-thirds majority vote within 10 days of declaration of martial law. However, if the Supreme Court overturns the President and Congress' decision then martial law must be lifted immediately. When considering supporting or denying the President's declaration of martial law, both the Congress and Supreme Court must consider whether declaration of martial law is the only way to restore order, and, secondarily, whether the President's plan to restore order is prudent and expeditious.

If it is believed by Congress or the Supreme Court that the declaration of martial law is prudent, but that the President's plan to remedy the crisis is not, the Supreme Court and Congress may support the declaration of martial law through appropriate means, but then require the President to submit a new proposal on how to remedy the crisis within 10 days of the Supreme Court or Congressional vote.

Also, the imposition of martial law can only temporarily suspend the following Inalienable Rights as spelled out in Article II: From Section1: The rights of People and legal residents of the CDA to peaceably assemble; Section 2: The right of the People to bear arms; Section 3: People and legal residents to be secure from unreasonable searches and seizures; Section 4: Right to trials for crimes; Section 5. Trials involving Military personnel in foreign countries; Section 8. Due process of the law; rules for use of torture, if warranted; Section 9. Rights of accused in criminal cases to a speedy jury trial; Section 10. Rights of participants in civil suits to a speedy judgment; Section 14. No seizure of private property for public use without just compensation; and Section 24. No Military personnel shall be housed, garrisoned or embedded with or among the People or legal residents of the CDA.

No other Sections in Article II will be subject to suspension, and, in no event, shall anyone suspend the People and legal residents' right to free speech, freedom of philosophy, and freedom of press. Also, even though Section 14 is allowed to be suspended during martial law, once martial law is lifted, the government must compensate the owner(s) of the private property that was used during martial law for the use, damage, destruction or loss of the said private property according to prices that were customary and dominant prior to the development of the emergency that led to the declaration of martial law, plus 10%.

Section 3. The Congress or the Supreme Court will also have the right to end martial law.

When declaring martial law, the President must also outline the objectives hoped to be achieved through the implementation of martial law. Once these objectives have been largely and generally achieved, the President must declare the end to the emergency and vacate martial law. However, if Congress or the Supreme Court through two-thirds majority believe that the end of martial law is appropriate each can independently and separately declare the end of martial law and the President and all branches of the government must comply.

Section 4. Abuse of Power of Martial Law shall result in the execution of the President, Vice President and the President's Cabinet.

If the President is found to have misused or abused the power to declare martial law by at least two-thirds of Congress and two-thirds of the Supreme Court than the President, Vice President and the members of the President's Cabinet that supported the imposition of martial law will be summarily executed by firing squad. Those in the President's Cabinet that opposed the declaration of martial law will be exempted from execution. In contrast, if martial law is declared by the President, supported by the Supreme Court and Congress, found to be prudent, and the implementation of martial law achieves the desired effect and objectives and martial law is ended in a timely fashion thereafter then the Cabinet members that were opposed to martial law will immediately resign from their positions and sent to prison for a minimum of 20 years with no pension benefits. However, if the President believes that any Cabinet member's opposition to martial law was with good intention and thoughtfulness then the President may pardon the said Cabinet member, but, regardless, the Cabinet member must still resign from all government position, never to return to any government service.

Article. II. Inalienable Rights of All People of the Constitutional Democracy of America

Section. 1. Freedom of Philosophy, speech, of the press, and right of petition.

Congress shall make no laws, regulations, rules, legislation, policy and the like with regard to or in consideration of any religious or philosophical doctrine. Congress shall make no law respecting an establishment of any Philosophy, including any religion, or prohibit the free exercise to believe in and practice any Philosophy, including any religion, as long as the belief and practice of said Philosophy, including any religion, does not bring physical or financial harm to others. Congress shall make no laws, regulations, rules, legislation, policy and the like that would in any way abridge the freedom of speech, or of the press; or the right of the residents of the CDA to assemble peaceably, and to petition the government for a redress of grievances. When legislating, regulating or establishing any rule of law, Congress shall not consider nor favor the doctrine or Philosophy of one or more groups over others, which could lead to prejudice, division or segregation in our society.

Section 2. Right of People to bear arms is not to be infringed.

A well-regulated militia, being necessary to the security of a free country, the right of the People to keep and bear any arms, shall not be infringed. However, Congress is entitled to make laws to register all weapons, magazines, ammunitions, explosive munitions, and owners regardless of type or kind of weapon, explosive munitions, and ammunition, the information to which shall be kept private and available only to law enforcement officers and other government authorities involved in domestic law enforcement, including investigations concerning terrorism, espionage and crime. All weapons and explosives munitions manufactured, imported or sold in the CDA will contain security measures and sold in a lockbox such that the only person who could access and use the weapon, ammunitions or explosives munitions would be the properly registered owner of the weapon, ammunitions or explosives munitions. All weapons, explosives munitions and lockbox will be manufactured with a global positioning system (GPS) device installed such that should the GPS device be incapacitated for whatever reason, the lockbox will be permanently locked and the weapon or explosives munitions will be rendered useless. GPS devices shall be left inactive unless activated by law enforcement officials either directly or remotely due to suspicion of the weapon or munitions being involved in a crime or at the request of the owner of the weapons or munitions due to theft. Law enforcement officials must obtain court authorization to enable any GPS system that is on a lockbox or weapon or explosive munitions; however, if law enforcement officials believe that time is of the essence then the law enforcement official may enable a GPS device with the permission of the department head and then obtain a court order to do so after the fact. However, if the courts rule that the enabling of the GPS device is unlawful then the GPS device must be immediate deactivated.

Section 3. People and legal residents to be secure from unreasonable searches and seizures.

The right of the People and legal residents to be secure in their persons, houses, papers, data, information, and effects, against unreasonable searches and seizures, shall not be violated, and no warrants shall be issued without reasonable probable cause, supported by oath or affirmation, and particularly describing the place to be searched, and the persons or things to be seized.

Section 4. Right to trials for crimes.

No person shall be held to answer for a capital or other crimes, unless presented with an indictment of a grand jury, except in cases arising in the Military, including the reserves, or in the national militia. When a person serving in the Military (including active duty reserve or militia personnel) is held to answer for a capital or other crimes, a courts-martial shall be convened to determine guilt or innocence, unless the alleged capital or other crimes happened while off duty during peace time, in a peaceful country or in a peaceable part of the country that is at war, in which case the Military personnel (including active duty reserve or militia personnel) will be subject to the same judicial process as any civilian Person of the CDA.

Section 5. Trials involving Military personnel in foreign countries.

When a Military personnel serving overseas is accused of capital or other crimes, the person in question will be subject to CDA Military justice when the capital or other crime was alleged to occur while the person was deemed to have been or should have been on duty, but subject to the host country's civil justice in all other situations, assuming that the host country's judicial system is based on a jury trial system and holds true to the Justice system where one is innocent until proven guilty. In such situations; the jury will consist of CDA Military personnel only, but vetted by both the defense attorney (CDA civilian or CDA military) and the host country's prosecuting attorney. The judge will also be a member of the CDA Military; however, the presiding judge will invite a host country judge to sit at the bench with the presiding judge and provide guidance, consultation and advice as deemed necessary by the presiding judge or when called for by the host country judge. All consultations between the judges will be made in the presence of both the prosecuting and defense attorneys. When rendering procedural judgment or ruling on objections, the presiding judge must consult and seek advice from the host country judge, and in the presence of both the prosecuting and defense attorneys.

If the foreign Justice system does not meet all conditions outlined above then the CDA Military shall convene a jury trial in the foreign country utilizing CDA civilian judicial rules and a CDA judge (who may be a member of the CDA Military), but with a jury consisting of citizens of the foreign country in which the CDA Military personnel is alleged to have committed a crime in. The CDA civilian judicial rules and procedures as well as the premise and history of those rules and procedures will be explained to the jury, so that the jury understands the nature of the CDA civilian judicial system. When explaining CDA's judicial system, care must be taken not to offend the sensibilities of the host country citizens nor diminishing the importance and effectiveness of the host country's judicial system. The potential jurors will be vetted by both the prosecuting and defense attorneys according to US civilian judicial rules, and once selected will be completely sequestered until a verdict is rendered, the judge declares a mistrial or the charges are dismissed. The process and selection of jurors will be completely kept secret and only the judge, and the lead prosecuting and lead defense attorneys will be privileged to the process and the information resulting from jury selection. While in jury selection, the judge, the lead prosecuting attorney and lead defense attorney will also be sequestered and only the judge will be allowed any contact with the outside world, and only as the outside contact is absolutely necessary. Also, CDA Military personnel will be the only ones allowed direct contact with the judge, but civilian authorities of the host country will be allowed to monitor the contact, including reasonable search of items passed back and forth from the judge to CDA Military personnel.

Section 6. Double jeopardy, hung jury, mistrials and five trial limit.

No Person or resident of the CDA subject to the CDA judicial system shall be subject to more than one trial that ends with a publicly announced jury verdict of guilt or innocence for the same alleged crime. However, if the trial does not end with a publicly announced jury verdict of guilt or innocence, the determination of whether or not to proceed with a second trial shall be left up to the prosecuting attorney. If the second trial also does not end with a publicly announced jury verdict of guilt or innocence, the determination of whether or not to convey a third trial will be made by the prosecuting attorney in consultation with the presiding judge in the second trial. If the third trial also ends with no publicly announced jury verdict of guilt or innocence then for the prosecuting attorney to convene a fourth trial, the prosecuting attorney must gain permission to do so from the Appellate Court. There will not be a fifth trial, unless the Supreme Court allows such judicial process to proceed.

In no event, under any circumstances, will a sixth or more trial be allowed to occur after five trials that ended with no publicly announced jury verdict of guilt or innocence, unless, jury tampering, or bribing or blackmailing of the judge can be proven in one or more of the trials, in which case the trial involving jury tampering or bribing or blackmailing of the judge will have deemed to have never occurred. Also, through a trial, if the prosecution is proven to have tampered with the jury or bribed or blackmailed the judge then the guilty parties – including those that turned a blind eye – will be terminated from their positions, and given a sentence that is to be the greater of 20 years in prison or the maximum sentence the accused in the original trial would have received, if found guilty, plus 5 years with no early parole. If the accused in the original trial was subject to the death penalty than the responsible parties in the prosecuting team accused of jury tampering or bribing or blackmailing the judge will be given the death sentence.

The trial of the accused criminal whose case involved jury tampering or bribing or blackmailing the judge by the prosecution will be reconstituted with replacement personnel and will start fresh with a new judge or jury or both. Otherwise, if the defense is proven to have tampered with the jury or bribed or blackmailed the judge through a trial then the guilty parties – including those that turned a blind eye – will be subject to immediate arrest and prosecution for maliciously interfering with the judicial process, and, if found guilty, subject to a maximum sentence applicable to the crimes that were alleged to have been committed in the original trial involving the jury tampering or bribing or blackmailing the judge by the defense plus five years. If the maximum sentence were to have been the death penalty in the original trial that resulted in findings of jury tampering or blackmailing or bribing the judge by the defense then the sentence for the crime of maliciously interfering with the judicial process shall also be the death penalty. In the case of a mistrial, the trial shall not be counted towards the five trial limit.

Section 7. No one shall be forced to bear witness against themselves.

No one shall be compelled or forced to be a witness against themselves or incriminate themselves in any criminal case.

Section 8. Due process of the law; rules for use of torture, if warranted.

No one shall be deprived of life, liberty, Income (includes all income, passive and active and capital gain), assets or properties, without due process of law that is a resident in the CDA or subject to CDA jurisdiction. Anyone arrested for a crime in the CDA or in a territory that is subject to CDA jurisdiction must be read their Miranda rights before being questioned, but not necessarily at the time of arrest, as long as it is administered within 48 hours of arrest and before questioning. No one that is a resident of the CDA or subject to CDA jurisdiction that is accused of a crime or espionage shall be tortured. Enemy nation combatants shall be treated with dignity and respect, and shall not be tortured. However, although enemies of the country that are deemed terrorists shall also be treated with dignity and respect, in general, if intelligence officers have probable cause to believe that certain prisoners – regardless of nationality and residence – have possession of time-sensitive and vital information to the safety and security of the CDA and its residents, the intelligence officers with clearance from the Judicial branch, and oversight of the legislative branch may employ whatever means necessary, in escalating steps with ample warning to the prisoner of what's to come, to acquire the information necessary to protect the CDA or its residents, including the sanctioned and authorized torture of the said prisoner.

Section 9. Rights of accused in criminal cases to a speedy jury trial.

In all criminal prosecutions, the accused shall enjoy the right to a speedy and public trial, by an impartial jury of the municipality wherein the crime shall have been alleged to have been committed, which municipality shall have been previously ascertained by law, and to be informed of the nature and cause of the accusation; to be confronted with the witnesses against the accused, to have compulsory process for obtaining witnesses in the accused person's favor, and to have the assistance of counsel for defense. However, should the presiding judge deem it necessary to relocate the trial to prevent premeditated prejudice towards the accused, the presiding judge will be given the latitude to make such a determination.

Section 10. Rights of participants in civil suits to a speedy judgment.

In all civil disputes, the disputed parties shall enjoy the right to a speedy and public trial, where provided for below, by an impartial jury of the municipality wherein the dispute shall deemed to have occurred, which municipality shall have been previously ascertained by law, and to be informed of the nature and cause of the dispute; to be confronted with all witnesses and testimony against the parties; to have compulsory process for obtaining witnesses and testimony in each party's favor, and to have the assistance of counsel for the trial.

In civil disputes, where the value in dispute shall exceed 25% of the average income of a Citizen of the CDA averaged over the last five years, the right of trial by jury shall be preserved, and no fact tried by a jury, shall be otherwise re-examined in any court of the CDA other than according to the rules of prevailing law and established precedent.

All results of jury trials will be made publicly available and announced by the court via print, internet, broadcast, media coverage and other broad communication channels, services, devices and the like. All results will be maintained by a central database under the jurisdiction of the Supreme Court and will be cross categorized such that information from results of the trials will be easy to search, research and mine for data.

Also, if all parties agree to arbitration then arbitration rules listed below will be followed. No compensation of any kind will be awarded to any party for choosing arbitration over jury trial.

In civil disputes, where the value in controversy shall not exceed 25% of the average income of a Citizen of the CDA averaged over the last five years, the right of trial by jury shall be made available, if one or more parties involved invoke their right to trial by jury, and no fact tried by a jury, shall be otherwise re-examined in any court of the CDA other than according to the rules of prevailing law and established precedent. If all parties waive their right to trial by jury, a Federally sanctioned neutral arbitration panel of a minimum of three members shall be convened to adjudicate the matter in question. Arbitration panelists shall be selected anonymously from a pool of qualified arbitration experts and will be paid by the Federal government who shall collect an additional amount of 10% of all awards resulting from jury trials, arbitration, and settlements, but 20% in cases of malfeasance, gross negligence or when conspiracy is proven (according to the standards of civil disputes, but not to the level of criminal disputes).

The pool of arbitrators shall be increased or decreased such that matters pending arbitration shall commence through the arbitration process with no more than a six month delay once the request for arbitration has been formally and correctly submitted. The request for arbitration shall not be unduly cumbersome nor require special assistance to complete by an average Citizen of the CDA.

All arbitration results including the reason for why the judgment was rendered for one party versus another will be made publicly available and announced by the arbitration panel via print, internet, broadcast, media coverage and other broad communication channels, services, devices and the like. All results will be maintained by a central database under the jurisdiction of the Supreme Court and will be cross categorized such that information from results of arbitration will be easy to search, research and mine for data.

Section 11. No settlements without a guilty plea will be allowed.

All disputes that are settled must require a guilty plea by the party that makes financial remuneration. Also, results of all settlements must be made publicly available and announced by the court or arbitration panel via print, internet, broadcast, media coverage and other broad communication channels, services, devices and the like. All results will be maintained by a central database under the jurisdiction of the Supreme Court and will be cross categorized such that information from results of the settlements will be easy to search, research and mine for data.

No party shall be allowed to make a financial settlement without a guilty plea. If the party that wants to pay a financial settlement refuses to enter any plea, guilty or otherwise, then the matter will be subject to a jury trial if the value of the controversy exceeds 25% of the average income of a Citizen of the CDA averaged over the last five years, unless all parties agree to arbitration. If the value of the controversy does not exceed 25% of the average income of a Citizen of the CDA averaged over the last five years then the dispute will be subject to arbitration, unless all parties involved want a jury trial. Regardless, the outcome of the jury trial or arbitration will be made publicly available and announced by the court or arbitration panel via print, internet, broadcast, media coverage and other broad communication channels, services, devices and the like.

Section 12. Bails, fines, and punishments shall be greater than the alleged or actual crime.

To actually deter crime, the punishments rendered to guilty parties in all cases (civil or criminal) shall be greater than the crime.

Punitive awards from jury trials and arbitration shall not be limited in cases of malfeasance, gross negligence or conspiracy in any way shape or form. In all other cases, punitive awards will be subject to judicial review by the presiding judge.

All bails and fines shall also be greater than the alleged crime or actual crime or violation.

Section 13. Special dispensation for premeditated murder and rape or sexual molestation of minors; amendment of statutory rape laws.

In direct-DNA evidenced cases of premeditated murder or where clear video or clear picture of the crime of premeditated murder of one or more individuals is presented as evidence, and it can be demonstrated that the evidence could not have been tampered with, if the accused is found guilty, the murderer will be sentence to death in the manner that most closely resembles the method the murderer used to kill the victims. In the case of rape of children or sexual abuse of children and where direct DNA or photographic or video evidence is also presented, and it can be demonstrated that the evidence could not have been tampered with, if the accused is found guilty, the rapist will have their genitals removed then given a choice of life in prison with no parole or, one year after having their genitals removed, death by impalement. In the case of rape of an adult, where direct DNA or photographic or video evidence is also presented, and it can be demonstrated that the evidence could not have been tampered with, if the accused is found guilty, the rapist will have their genitals removed and sent to prison for at least 25 years with no parole.

All statutory rape laws will be suspended in cases where both parties are under-18 years of age and where there was mutual consent or where both parties were under-18 years of age when they started having sexual relations, but one party became 18 before another and there was mutual consent. In all other cases, involving the sexual relation of a minor, the court or jury must determine whether there was true informed consent between the parties, or if it was a coerced consent or if the minor was incapable of rendering an independent and informed judgment. Statutory rape laws shall apply to both male and female victims equally.

Section 14. Slavery prohibited.

Neither slavery nor involuntary servitude of any kind, including any forced extraction of wealth from one Person for the benefit of another, redistribution of wealth, or other forced obligation of one Person or People for the benefit of another Person or People will be allowed or shall exist within the CDA, or any place subject to CDA jurisdiction.

Section 15. Reserved rights of People.

Any rights guaranteed in the Constitution shall not be construed to cancel, deny, limit, restrict, curb, curtail, disparage, suspend or the like any other rights granted by the Constitution or cancel, deny, limit, restrict, curb, curtail, disparage, suspend or the like other rights retained by the People.

Section 16. No seizure of private property for public use without just compensation.

Private property shall not be taken for public use without just compensation – just compensation will be the greater of an appraised value, fair market value, or comparable value, excluding winning speculative bids in anticipation of government confiscation, plus 10%.

Section 17. Income tax rates shall never exceed more than 20% and a national sales tax shall never exceed 5%.

Total income tax collected by the Federal government through the Internal Revenue Service (or its successor and assigns) shall never exceed more than 20% of any individual's income under any circumstances and a national sales tax shall never exceed 5% of the purchase price of an item or service. However, as prescribed in this document, four temporary surcharges will be allowed under strict regulation and oversight. These four items will be limited to the following: 1) For the reduction of Federal government debt to Allowable Limits, 2) For legally permitted disaster recovery, 3) For legally permitted emergency stimulus spending, or 4) For funding of wars above and beyond the peacetime military budget. A surcharge tax will be collected directly from payment of an individual's compensation from salaries, wages, and income or through a national sales tax.

Section 18. No other taxes allowed other than Income and Sales taxes.

No other taxes shall be collected. Specifically, no taxes shall be collected on capital gains, corporate income, interest income, dividends, inheritance, gifts, charitable donations, pensions, retirement accounts, tax on civil or criminal settlements (other than allowed surcharges to pay for the judicial process, including maintenance of arbitrators), insurance proceeds or from income from gambling, unless the individual makes their primary income from gambling or declares their profession to be a gambler. Taxes on interest, dividend and capital gains will be collected as if it were like wages and salary, if the person's primary source of income is from investments. The investor rule on income taxes will not apply to those individuals that are retired. No Federal government employees will be required to pay income taxes, including all teachers (pre-K to 12th grade) working at Federally funded schools and professors and lecturers of colleges, universities, and all graduate, doctoral and post-doctoral programs that are funded by the Federal government. No marriage penalty shall exist, and every individual will be taxed as individuals.

Section 19. Income tax, due date and reporting.

Everyone that has an income must pay income taxes, unless specifically exempted in this document. All income taxes are to be paid by no later than January 31 for the prior calendar year. In addition, also by January 31, each individual that has an income must also file an income tax report. All individuals must pay at least the same rate of income taxes, if not the same amount. So called progressive taxes or any variation there of shall never be permitted. All income tax forms will be no more than 12 lines long: 1) Salary, wages, income, fees, bonuses, 2) tips, 3) interest income, excluding qualified tax-free interest income, 4) capital gain, excluding qualified tax-free capital gain, 5) income from dividends, excluding qualified tax-free dividends, 6) income from gambling, if required, 7) other income or revenue, 8) Total Personal Revenue, 9) applicable tax rate, 10) taxes due, 11) taxes paid, and 12) difference due for payment or difference due for refund. Capital gains, interest income and dividends will be taxed as regular income for individuals whose primary source of income is from investments – e.g., investors, wealthy individuals, professionals working in the asset/investment/money/portfolio management business. However, interest, dividend and capital gains derived from a retirement plan shall not be taxed even for professionals in the investment industry, and retirees will not be required to pay taxes on capital gains, interest income and dividends. No estate, inheritance, gift taxes or the like will be permitted to exist or to be collected. Monies from direct-line family members will not be treated as income and will not be taxed, e.g., grandparents to grandchildren, children to parents, parents to children, brothers to sisters, sisters to brothers, but not between cousins.

Section 20. Piercing the veil

When determining the taxability of a source of income for an individual, the IRS will ignore the labeling of the income source and will look to the origination of the income to determine the taxability of the income to the individual. In general, when interpreting the Constitution, legislations, laws, rules, regulations or the like, the Judicial Branch shall ignore the semantics of language and will "pierce the veil" to the true purpose, meaning, condition, result, intention, method, process, thesis, and the like to determine Justice, fairness, legality, Constitutionality, and the like in all Judicial, legislative, and administrative dealings.

Section 21. Prohibition on immoral and unjust laws, including quotas of any kind, and so called progressive taxes.

Congress shall make no law that is immoral or unjust and any law that is proven immoral or unjust shall be immediately suspended then revoked by the President of the Constitutional Democracy of America. Congress shall make no laws, rules, regulations and the like that benefit one group of People at the expense of another. Congress shall make no laws, rules, regulations and the like that prejudices or discriminates against one group or another. Congress shall make no laws, rules, regulations and the like that separates or divides one group versus another. Therefore, no quotas of any kind shall be allowed in any organization, business, institution, educational establishment, charity, NGO, club, group or the like that are subject to CDA jurisdiction. Also, therefore, so called progressive taxes will never be allowed.

Section 22. Voting limited to Citizens.

Only Citizens of the CDA 21 years old and older will be allowed to vote in any election, Federal or local, assuming that the individual is qualified to do so.

Section 23. Citizenship defined; privileges of citizens.

All persons born or naturalized in the CDA will be Citizens of the CDA, have the option to be Citizens of the CDA or will have the option to set upon the path to become a Citizen of the CDA, subject to conditions outlined in the Definitions section of this document. No municipality shall make or enforce any law which shall abridge the rights, privileges or immunities of Citizens of the CDA; nor shall any municipality deprive any person of life, liberty, Income, asset or property, without due process of law; nor deny to any person within its jurisdiction the equal protection of laws and the Constitution.

Section 24. Writ of Habeas Corpus shall not be suspended without due cause.

The privilege of the Writ of Habeas Corpus shall not be suspended, unless in cases of rebellion or invasion and the public safety requires it. The suspension of the Writ of Habeas Corpus will be instituted by the President, but the Congress may challenge this decision by the President with a simple majority vote at which point the Supreme Court will determine the Constitutionality of the suspension imposed by the President.

Section 25. No bill of attainder or ex post facto law.

No bill of attainder or ex post facto law shall be passed.

Section 26. No Military personnel shall be housed, garrisoned or embedded with or among the People or legal residents of the CDA.

The CDA government's Military shall not be used against the people living in the CDA, or garrisoned in civilian communities, unless the mayor of a city or Member of Congress requests the presence of the Military of the CDA to help with quelling an insurrection, disaster recovery, or other emergencies or legally mandated martial law is declared and enforced as prescribed according to the procedures outlined in this document.

Section 27. Right to marriage.

Regardless of sexual orientation, all individuals residing in the territorial borders of the CDA or subject to the jurisdiction of the CDA will be entitled to marry whomever they wish, but will only be allowed one marriage at a time. Accordingly, regardless of whether the couple is heterosexual, homosexual or any other combination, all legally married couples will be accorded exactly the same rights.

Section 28. Pregnant female's right to choose.

All pregnant females that are sixteen (16) years of age or older will have the right to choose whether they wish to give birth or abort the pregnancy without consultation or consent of any other individual; however, the choice to abort the pregnancy and the actual conscious act of abortion must take place prior to the expiration of 100 days of pregnancy – the determination of when the end of the 100 day period is reached must be determined by the woman's doctor. No one will be permitted to interfere with the woman's decision in either direction. Females under the age of 16 will also be allowed to choose whether they wish to give birth or abort the pregnancy, but the decision must be made in conjunction and in consultation with the female's parent(s) or primary caretaker(s). If the female under the age of 16 wishes to have an abortion, but the parents of the female or the parents of the male who impregnated the female wishes to have the baby born then the parents of the female or the parents of the male who impregnated the female will have the right to have the baby born. However, if such an intervention is exercised, the party who intervened to have the baby born must take 100% of the responsibility to raise the new born to adulthood, which at this time is 18 years of age. The interveners will also determine, what if any role the female who gave birth or the male who impregnated the female will have in raising the newborn. However, neither the female who gave birth nor the male that impregnated the female is obligated to assume any role. If the female is under the age of 16, but the male is expected to be 18 or older at the time of birth then the male will have the option to also intervene and take possession of the new born and exercise his responsibility as a father until the baby reaches 18 years of age. The only exception to the last rule will be in the case of rape, in which case the male will not have any say in determining the future of the pregnancy.

Section 29. Right to termination.

Each individual has the right to end their life in any manner that they see fit other than to do so in a public area or public manner, do so in a way that endangers others, do so in a way that inconveniences others or do so, if under the age of 18 years old. If electing to terminate one's own life, the individual must make arrangements for their corpse to be properly removed and buried or cremated, prior to ending one's life.

Section 30. No morality laws shall exist for any Person that is deemed an adult.

Each adult Person shall have the right to engage in the following activities as long as it is consensual and does not endanger or bring physical or financial harm to others: Prostitution, gambling, and drug use, including alcohol and tobacco. No other morality laws shall be permitted to exist. No children shall engage or be allowed to engage by their parents, legal guardian or any adult, in any act of prostitution, gambling or drug use and shall not be allowed to be used or exploited in any manner deemed inappropriate by the child or their parents or legal guardian.

Section 31. No traffic laws will be allowed to exist only traffic recommendations, but the consequences of any accident shall be handled based on existing criminal law.

All traffic laws will be suspended. All existing traffic rules shall be maintained, but for informational purposes for the public. However, anyone causing an accident shall be held responsible for the consequences of the accident. Therefore, as an example, if a driver is found guilty of killing another person or persons through negligence, mishandling, poor judgment or preventable mistake under reasonable circumstances then the driver will be tried for voluntary manslaughter or murder depending on the circumstances. Another example: If the driver is found guilty of injuring another person or persons through negligence, mishandling, poor judgment or preventable mistake under reasonable circumstances then the driver will be tried for assault with a deadly weapon. If the driver is found to have been intoxicated or otherwise under the influence of alcohol or chemicals that are deemed inappropriate for drivers to consume while operating a vehicle and found guilty, the penalty shall be doubled. However, regardless of the state of the driver, if there is a reasonable doubt that the accident was not the fault of the driver then no criminal charges will be levied against the driver.

Article III. Restrictions on government employees and retirees' activities.

Section 1. Disqualifications to hold government office.

No Citizen shall qualify to stand for election or hold office as President or Vice President, a Member of Congress, or hold any government positions, civil or military, under the CDA, or under any municipality, who shall have been convicted of engaging in insurrection or rebellion against the CDA, or given aid or comfort to the enemies of the CDA or have been convicted of a crime or had a negative judgment rendered in a civil suit against the individual or against an organization that the individual was a member and had management control over or was a member of the board of directors.

Section 2. No former Federal employee shall work as a lobbyist or for a for-profit business.

No former employee of the Federal government whether in the Executive, Legislative or Judicial Branch of the government, elected or otherwise, including Military personnel that have obtained the rank of Lieutenant Colonel, Commander or the equivalent and higher, shall work as a lobbyist, advocate, consultant, advisor or the like and shall not work for any for-profit organizations, enterprises, businesses or the like.

Section 3. Federal employees will not be permitted to invest in individual securities.

No Federal employee, elected or otherwise, will be allowed to invest in individual securities. All Federal employees, elected or otherwise, will only be allowed to invest in broad indices, but in no way directly or indirectly in indices of industries that the Federal employee had or has oversight, connection, relation, affiliation, or the like. And former Federal employees, elected or otherwise, will be under the same restrictions as current Federal employees for up to ten (10) years after retirement or leaving office.

Also, once the former Federal employee, elected or otherwise, invests in or owns individual securities, the individual will never be allowed to stand for any election for any government office and shall never be allowed to return to working for the government in any capacity or be involved in advising, counseling, lobbying, campaigning for, or the like any government official, elected or otherwise, or government organizations, agencies, departments, groups, or the like.

Section 4. Meetings involving Politicians shall be publicly broadcast and recorded, except for meetings involving national security.

All meetings involving Politicians (those that have to be elected to office) Federal or Municipal, Cabinet members, their staff, aides, direct reports or the like, whether with other Politicians, Cabinet members their staff, aides, direct reports or the like, or with lobbyists, advisors, consultants, advocates or the like, constituents, or with foreign officials, executive, legislative or judicial, will be publicly broadcast and recorded and a database of these meetings will be stored in a central location for posterity for the next one thousand (1,000) years, shall be made available to the general public at any time, and shall be supervised and monitored under the purview of the Supreme Court of the CDA. The database will be properly organized, categorized and otherwise maintained to make it as easy as possible to search, research and mine data.

Exceptions shall be made for meetings regarding national or municipal security issues and matters: National and municipal security meetings will be recorded, stored and organized in exactly the same manner as all other meetings; however, meetings dealing with national or municipal securities matters will not be made available to the general public until the veil of national or municipal security is lifted according to established protocols, which Congress will establish and the Supreme Court will approve.

Any government employee, Federal or Municipal, that violates monitoring rules outlined in this section of the Constitution will be removed from their positions, will be required to refund all of the compensation that was earned during their employment with the Federal or municipal government, plus interest, will forfeit all of their retirement and pension benefits, and will be sentenced to prison for a minimum of 20 years without parole. Regarding this matter, all Politicians, Cabinet members, their staff, aides, direct reports or the like will be presumed to be guilty until proven innocent. This will be the only situation in which the judicial principle of "guilty until proven innocent" will be enforced.

Section 5. Annual mental competency test required for select government officials.

No government official will be permitted to serve, if the government official is determined to suffer from dementia, Alzheimer's or similar physical afflictions. Every key government official will undergo annual tests for dementia, Alzheimer's or similar physical afflictions. Government officials subject to the annual test must include but not limited to the President, Vice-President,

Members of Congress, Cabinet Members, Supreme, Appellate, and District Court Justices, Flag Officers in the Military, key department heads such as the Director of the CIA, Director of the FBI, Head of the EPA, IRS, Agency and Bureau heads and the like.

All of the same government officials that are subject to dementia, Alzheimer's or similar physical afflictions tests will also be subject to mental illness and mental competency tests.

Article IV. Compensation, benefits and pension for Federal government employees.

Section 1. Tax-free compensation, benefits, and pensions.

Since monetary compensation for all Federal employees are drawn from income tax receipts, compensation, benefits and pensions for Federal employees will be provided free of Federal income taxes.

Section 2. Compensation for Federal government employees.

The President, Vice President and Justices of the Supreme Court will receive a monthly financial compensation not to exceed five times the average monthly income of all Citizens over the previous five (5) years. Members of the President's Cabinet, Congress and Flag Officers of the Military will receive a monthly financial compensation not to exceed three times the average monthly income of all Citizens over the previous five (5) years. All other Federal government employees will be given a bi-monthly compensation, which shall not exceed two-and-a-half times the average bi-monthly income of all Citizens over the previous five years. For the President, Vice President, Cabinet Members and Members of Congress only, half of their annual compensation shall be withheld for five-years and thereafter paid out over five years. However, the payout shall depend on the economic performance of the CDA. To measure the economic performance of the CDA, three economic statistics will be considered: 1) Inflation, 2) unemployment, and 3) interest rate. For the President, Vice President, Cabinet Members and Members of Congress to get full refund of their withheld compensation, 1) the average rate of inflation over the previous five years must not exceed 1.5% nor fall into deflation, 2) the average unemployment rate over the last five years must not rise above 5%, and 3) the average interest rate on the 10 federal government bond must not exceed 3%. If the CDA experiences a deflationary environment at any time during the measurement period or the average five-year inflation rate exceeds 2.5%, as declared by the Federal Reserve Bank and verified by at least 50 reputable academic institutions and think tanks of varied political spectrum then all withheld compensation shall be forfeit. If the CDA experiences an average unemployment rate of greater than 6% during the previous five years as declared by the Federal Reserve Bank and verified by at least 50 reputable academic institutions and think tanks of varied political spectrum then all withheld compensation shall be forfeit. If the CDA experiences an average interest rate on the 10-year federal government bond of greater than 4.5% during the previous five years as determined by the bond markets then all withheld compensation shall be forfeit. At all other times, the withheld compensation that is the subject of potential refund in any given year shall be split into three equal pieces and each third shall be assigned to each of the performance measures – Inflation, unemployment and interest rate – to determine the amount of the refund. The amount of the refund shall be calculated on a linear basis from 100% to 0% based on the goal posts set above. For inflation, the goal posts are 1.5% to 2.5%, for unemployment it is 5%-6%, and for the 10-year government bond rate it is 3%-4.5%.

Section 3. Travel, food and lodging expenses.

Each qualified Federal employee including the President, Vice President, Cabinet members, Members of Congress, Flag Officers and others that are designated by the President, approved by Congress and sanctioned by the Supreme Court Justices as qualified shall be allowed expenses for travel, lodging and food for business related to the government of the CDA. In addition, the President, Vice President, Cabinet members, and Members of Congress will be allowed two all expenses paid trips back home per year for the employee and their immediate household (people that live under one roof that are related). When considering expenses, all travel, lodging and food shall be what an average Citizen would pay for in the course of their lives. The only exception to this rule will be for the use of Military aircraft for official business of the CDA for only the President, Vice President, Cabinet members, Members of Congress and Flag Officers, including the presidential airplane, which shall be kept up to date with all of the latest communications devices, and, where appropriate, defensive capabilities. The presidential aircraft will be replaced no more than once every 25 years. For the President, Vice President, Cabinet members, the leaders of Congress, and Flag Officers, when traveling, consideration for the physical security of these members of government will be paramount in considering their mode of transportation and lodging. The Secret Service will have the sole discretion to determine the proper safety measures necessary to secure the physical well-being of the President, Vice President, Cabinet members, the leaders of Congress and Flag Officers.

Section 4. Health care benefits.

All Federal government employees, elected or otherwise, will be given the exact same medical, dental and optical benefits that shall cover not only the employee, but also their immediate family members (including spouse, husband, wife, life partner, and children), and all ancestors and descendants that do not have their own medical, dental or optical insurance. This benefit will also extend to honorably-retired Federal employees, elected or otherwise.

Section 5. Pension and retirement benefits.

All honorably retired Federal government employees, elected or otherwise, will be given a pension. The pension will vary with their time of service and last position in government. For employees of the Executive, Legislative and Judicial Branches that are not specifically detailed in this Section, an employee must have served at least five years to qualify for a pension. The pension would start at 12% of their last year of compensation and escalate on a linear basis to as high as 90% of the last full year's compensation for 40 years of service. For the President and Vice President, their pension shall be 10% of their initially authorized starting salary upon confirmation of their election. Thereafter, for every year in Office their pension will escalate at 10% of the salary for the year that they served. For Cabinet Members (including Director of the FBI, Director of the CIA, Chairman of the Federal Reserve Bank, Chairman of the FCC, the Head of the SEC, all Bureau and Agency heads and like institutions) and Flag Officers of the Military, pensions shall start at 25% of their initially authorized starting salary upon their confirmation by Congress then jump to 55% of their last full year of compensation for the first year of service and will increase linearly to as high as 75% for five years of service and then increase linearly to 90% for ten years of service. After completion of 15 years or more of service, the pension of the Members of Cabinet and Flag Officers shall increase to 100% of their last full year of service. For Members of Congress to qualify for a pension, they have to serve at least one year in Congress, which would initiate their pension at 22% of the last full year salary, which then escalates to as high as and limited to 100% for 40 years of service (10 terms). Members of the Supreme Court will receive the same pension benefits as the President. Appellate Judges will receive 80% of the pension benefits of the Justices of the Supreme Court, while District Court Judges will receive 60% of the pension benefits of the Justices of the Supreme Court.

Section 6. No other responsibilities or compensations.

No government employee shall have any other duties, responsibilities, jobs, activities, positions, affiliations or the like other than their full-time responsibilities as a government employee and as a volunteer for not-for-profit charities, if the government official so chooses to volunteer. As such, no government official shall receive compensation, remunerations, benefits or the like for anything other than performing the duties and responsibilities required of their government position.

Section 7. No gifts allowed to be received by any government official.

No government official will be allowed to receive any gift of any value from anyone. The only exception will be a gift of immaterial value as an exchange of courtesy with foreign dignitaries according to protocol.

Section. 8. Pay raises for all Federal employees shall not take effect until two elections of Members of Congress have passed.

No law, varying the compensation for the services of Federal employees shall take effect, until two elections (i.e., after two years) of Members of Congress shall have intervened.

Article V. The formation and governance of the Constitutional Democracy of America.

Section. 1. No states shall exist.

No states and state governments shall exist, be reconstituted, resurrected or otherwise created: Only the Federal government and municipal governments shall exist. All state institutions, agencies, functions, departments, and all other similar groups will be either disbanded or absorbed by the Federal or local governments as determined by Congress and the President.

Section. 2. Governance of the country, where appropriate, shall be conducted through direct and popular vote.

All Federal and local elections shall be determined by direct and popular vote only. Election for President and Vice President shall be held once every five (5) years on the second Tuesday of November in every year that ends in zero (0) or five (5). Election for Members of Congress shall occur on the second Tuesday of every November every year; however, in any given annual election, only one-quarter (25%) of the Congressional Districts will hold elections to choose a Member of Congress. Each Congressional District will select a Member of Congress only once every four (4) years. Every year, the Congressional Districts that are subject to elections will be spread evenly across the territorial boundaries of the CDA.

Section 3. Washington, District of Columbia will be maintained as the capital of the CDA.

Washington DC will be maintained as the capital of the Constitutional Democracy of America, where in all Federal government functions will reside, including all aspects of the Executive, Legislative and Judicial functions of the Federal government.

Article. VI. Powers, and duties of the President.

Section. 1. Office of the President shall be the Executive Power of the CDA; and process for electing the President and Vice President.

The Executive Power of the CDA shall be vested in the Office of the President. Each term for President shall be for five years, and, together with the Vice President, shall be elected as follows:

1) Each political party choosing to nominate a candidate for President will establish their own rules for nominating candidates;
2) Each candidate running for President will select their own candidate for Vice-President;
3) The election of President and Vice-President will be through direct popular vote. Only legal Citizens of the CDA that are at least 21 years old that are mentally competent will be permitted to vote in any national and local elections; and

4) No person except a natural born Citizen shall be eligible to be elected to the Office of President or Vice-President, must be at least forty five (45) years old, and must have been at least twenty-five (25) years a resident within the territorial boundaries of the CDA as of the day of election.

In case of an unexpected or unplanned vacancy of the Office of the POTCDA, the Vice-President will assume the position of President. If the Vice-President is unable to do so for whatever reason, then the Speaker of Congress shall be next in line followed by the Majority Leader of the Congress, followed by the Secretary of State, Secretary of Defense, Secretary of the Treasury, and Secretary of the Interior. The succession line thereafter will be determined by Congress.

Before the President-elect and Vice-President-elect qualify for their respective Offices, both must take the following Oath of Affirmation:--"I, (name), do solemnly swear that I will faithfully execute the Office of the President (or Vice President) of the Constitutional Democracy of America, and will to the best of my ability, preserve, protect and defend the Constitution of the Constitutional Democracy of America." The Oath of Affirmation taken by every federal employee will be done so with the left hand placed on the Constitution – including any amendments -- while the right is held at face level and the palm facing in the same direction as the face. The Oath of Affirmation for the President and the Vice President shall be administered by the Chief Justice of the Supreme Court in two separate ceremonies, while the Oath of Affirmation for all other elected Federal employees will be administered by a consenting judge chosen by the individual that is to take the Oath of Affirmation. Oath of Affirmation for all other Federal employees will be administered by the person's direct supervisor/manager. For example, in the case of the President's Cabinet Members, the oath of Affirmation will be administered by the President of the CDA.

Section. 2. Powers, duties and responsibilities of the President.

The President shall be the Commander in Chief of Economic Leadership and will be responsible for monitoring the economy and making sure that the Federal government is not only encouraging long-term economic growth, but also not getting in the way of it. The President shall do so by making sure that the Federal government promotes sound long-term economic policies and works towards removing barriers that hinder long-term economic growth of the Constitutional Democracy of America. In addition, the President shall ensure that economic policy of the Federal government is fair and Just to all at all times.

Also, as the Commander in Chief of Economic Leadership, the President will ensure that the Federal government does not own, administrate, interfere with, run, oversee, manage, dictate to, manipulate or the like any private-sector businesses, organizations, institutions, and the like, at any time, for any reason, no exceptions other than through legal, Just, moral and fair legislative and regulatory oversight.

The President shall be Commander in Chief of the Military of the CDA. As such, the President will have the power to deploy the Military forces of the CDA to any part of the world (or the universe as it becomes relevant) as the President sees fit and necessary for the security of the CDA. The President will also have the right to convene Congress to petition the Congress to declare war on another nation or foreign organization. The petition to declare war in front of Congress must come within 100 days of the President ordering the Military forces of the CDA to deploy as part of the war that the President is requesting from Congress. When petitioning Congress to declare war, the President must make clear the objectives hoped to be achieved and the time frame needed to achieve those objectives and the reasons for attempting to achieve those objectives. Congress shall not unreasonably withhold approval for war. After the President petitions Congress to declare war, Congress will have 50 days to act on the President's petition and must vote on the petition within that timeframe.

The President may require the opinion, in writing, of the principal officer or head of each of the Executive Departments, upon any subject relating to the duties of their respective Offices.

The President shall have the power to grant reprieves and pardons for offences against the CDA, but may not pardon one self.

The President shall have the power to conduct foreign affairs and execute foreign policy, including negotiating treaties with foreign countries and powers. However, in no event, shall the CDA ever negotiate with whom the CDA deem to be terrorists or terrorist organizations. In the course of conducting foreign policy, once the President has negotiated any treaty, a simple majority of Congress must approve the treaty to ratify it and make it legal and binding on the CDA, its government, and its People.

The President shall also nominate all Ambassadors, Consuls General and Consuls to foreign countries, heads of Executive Departments (formerly known as Department Secretary), Supreme, Appellate, and District Court Justices, and all other Officers of the CDA, including Military Generals, Admirals, and other

Flag Officers, but to be confirmed in those positions, the Congress must approve the nomination by majority vote, except Supreme Court nominations, which shall be approved by three-quarters of Congress. However, lesser Executive Department or Military positions shall be nominated and approved by the President, Executive Department heads or Courts of law as appropriate and necessary.

The President shall also receive all foreign Ambassadors and other senior most officials, including Prime Ministers, Presidents and Royalty. However, the President may delegate greeting of lesser foreign officials to subordinates, including any member of the President's Cabinet, the Vice President, Justices of the Supreme Court or the senior most Flag Officers of the Military, as appropriate. No President, Vice-President, Members of Congress, Supreme Court Justices and highest ranking Flag Officers of the CDA will subordinate themselves to any other country's leadership, while keeping in mind and observing all of the necessary protocols. Bowing to any foreign leader, pledging allegiance to any other country or leadership, or subordinating the sovereignty, integrity and independence of the CDA to any other country in any manner, gesture, posture, motion, hint or the like or in words, visually, or in any other forms of communication is strictly and absolutely forbidden.

Should an economic recession or worse be declared by a reputable and known third party entity or organization and confirmed by at least two other reputable and known independent organizations (which may include the Federal Reserve Bank), the President may choose to declare a state of economic emergency. If so declared, the President, along with advice from the Cabinet (composed of Executive Department heads) and Congress, and with input from the Internal Revenue Service, shall structure an Emergency Economic Spending Plan (EESP). The approval process necessary for the EESP to be implemented must follow the procedures detailed in this document.

Should a natural disaster occur, the President may choose to declare a state of emergency. If so declared, the President, along with advice from the Cabinet and Congress, and with input from the Internal Revenue Service, shall structure a Natural Disaster Recovery Spending Plan (NDRSP). The approval process necessary for the NDRSP to be implemented must follow the procedures detailed in this document.

The President must propose an annual balanced budget for the Federal government by October 31st (if October 31st is a Saturday or a Sunday then by the following Monday) of every year for the following calendar year, which must be approved by majority vote of Congress by February 15th of the year in which the budget is for (if February 15th is a Saturday or a Sunday then by the following Monday). Once the budget is submitted by the President, amendments and changes to the Federal budget may be proposed by the leaders of Congress or the President.

The President must lead the country at all times and must steer a course for the country that the President believes is the best course for all generations to come and pronounce a vision for the future that is at least one generation ahead. The President must also layout a plan on how to achieve these objectives, how to raise funds to achieve these policies and what the President believes the outlined policy would achieve, who it would benefit and why this is for the direct benefit of the country as a whole.

The President may recall any and all Members of Congress back to Washington and compel Congress to debate and vote on an issue that the President believes is important to resolve as expeditiously as possible. The procedure for the recall of Congress must follow the steps outlined in this document. However, once in session, the President may not disband Congress.

Section. 3. Annual state of the CDA address.

On an annual basis, the President shall deliver, in front of Congress, a State of the CDA speech in which the President outlines the progress towards the future vision over the last one year, what the President envisions for the remainder of the President's term, and connect it to the President's vision for future generations. The President may propose, for the consideration of Congress, new policies and recommendations that the President deems necessary to effectively execute policy for the benefit of all People, how the President expects it to be funded and why this proposed new policy is for the direct benefit of every Person.

Section 4. Appointments during Congressional Recess.

The President may make appointments to vacant government positions during Congressional recess; however, the appointments shall be temporary. Once Congress reconvenes, Presidential appointees will have to be confirmed by Congress in order for the temporary status of their appointment to be officially recognized and made permanent until the official resigns, retires, becomes incapacitated, dies in office, is fired, there's a change in administration or is impeached.

Section. 5. Removal of Officers upon criminal conviction.

The President, Vice President and all civil and Military Officers of the CDA, shall be removed from their respective Offices on impeachment for, and conviction of, treason, bribery, or other criminal offenses under Federal or local government law.

Article VII. The make-up, duties, responsibilities, and privileges of Congress.

Section 1. The make-up of Congress.

The Congress of the Constitutional Democracy of America shall only have one chamber referred to as Congress, and elected officials of Congress shall be referred to as Member or Members of Congress. The Senate of the United States of America will be dissolved and all Senators of the United States of America shall be transitioned to a Member of Congress in the CDA.

Section. 2. Election of Members of Congress.

Members of Congress shall be composed of elected officials chosen every fourth year from among only Citizens of the CDA. Citizens running for any government office shall have no criminal or civil convictions, or any settlements against them. To stand for election to become a Member of Congress, an individual must be at least forty (40) years old on the day of election, been at least fifteen (15) years a Citizen of the CDA, and a resident of the Congressional District from which the Member is to be selected for at least five (5) years.

Section 3. Alternate Members of Congress.

With each election for Members of Congress, the winner from each Congressional District shall assume the position of Member of Congress. In addition, the Citizen that came in second place shall be designated as an Alternate Member of Congress. However, the Alternate Member of Congress shall not become a Member of Congress unless the Citizen currently serving as the Member of Congress is fired for their inability to balance the Federal budget – this shall be the only time an Alternate Member of Congress shall assume the responsibilities as a Member of Congress. If the current Member of Congress ran unopposed then the elected Members of Congress from the opposing parties to the elected Member of Congress who ran unopposed will select an Alternate Member of Congress for the District that produced a Member of Congress who ran unopposed.

Section 4. No one running for Member of Congress.

In the event that no Citizen runs for Congress in a given Congressional District then a randomly selected Citizen shall serve as a Member of Congress and will be referred to as a Selected Member of Congress. The Selected Member of Congress shall receive all of the benefits, rights and privileges of an elected Member of Congress and shall have the same duties, responsibilities, and obligations, but will receive the greater of three times the pay of an elected Member of Congress or 200% of the average of the most recent five-year earnings of the selected Citizen as an annual salary and shall be required to serve the longer of four years or until the second scheduled election for Member of Congress for the Congressional District the Selected Member was selected from have passed. Therefore, during the time of the Selected Member of Congress' term, the first scheduled election for Member of Congress that would have taken place shall be suspended. However, the second scheduled election during the Selected Member of Congress' term shall be conducted, and the winner of that election shall be the new Member of Congress and shall replace the Selected Member of Congress in Congress. During the time of their service as a Selected Member of Congress, the individual must follow all of the rules, regulations, and laws that are required of elected Members of Congress. After the Selected Member of Congress successfully and honorably completes their term, they will be entitled to three-hundred (300) times the average income of a Citizen of the CDA as a one-time pension, tax-free, unless the individual chooses to run for the position for which they were selected and they win then they will not receive the retirement bonus and will be treated the same as all other Members of Congress.

Section 5. Congressional District, qualifications, vacancies, governance, and timing of elections.

The total number of Members of Congress shall be no more than one (1) Congressional Member for every 500,000 Citizens. Washington, District of Columbia (DC) shall have the same representation as all other municipalities in Congress and Citizens of Washington DC shall participate in all other Federal elections equally to all other Citizens of the CDA. Each Congressional District shall be geographically contiguous and its geographic shape will be the simplest form it can take and the number of persons in each Congressional District shall be approximately the same and shall not deviate by more than one-percent from one Congressional District to any other.

When vacancies occur in Congressional representation due to impeachment, death, illness, or incapacity, the Members of the party from which the vacancy occurred shall temporarily assign a Member from the Congressional District to represent said Congressional District until the term of the vacated Member is ended at which time a duly elected Member from the Congressional District shall replace the temporary Member. The temporary Member may choose to run for the office in which the temporary Member was assigned.

The Members of Congress shall choose their Speaker and other Officers. However, the Vice President of the CDA will be the Leader of Congress. If no one accepts the honor of leadership in Congress then a randomly selected individual from among the Members will serve in the leadership position that was left vacant.

Each Member of Congress shall have one vote. In the case of a tie, the Vice President of the Constitutional Democracy of America shall cast the tie-breaking vote.

Section 6. Term limits for Members of Congress

No Member of Congress shall serve more than ten (10) terms. Regardless, Members of Congress will be required to retire 10 years before the average life expectancy of the average Person of the same gender as the Member of Congress. [Comment: At current life expectancies, no Person will be able to serve 10 terms; however, as life expectancy increases the 10 term maximum rule should come into force.]

Section 7. Members of Congress shall be subject to all laws, regulations, rules and the like

Members of Congress shall be subject to all of the same laws, regulations and rules and the like as ordinary People of the CDA, unless specifically carved out by the Constitution.

Section 8. Impeachment powers of Congress

Congress will have the sole right of Impeachment of the President, Vice President and Supreme, Appellate, or District Court Justices. Congress shall also conduct the trial for the Impeachment of the President, Vice President and Supreme, Appellate, or District Court Justices. When the President, Vice President or a Supreme, Appellate or District Court Justice of the CDA is impeached, all Members of Congress must be present. When the President or Vice President is impeached, the Chief Justice of the Supreme Court of the CDA shall preside over the impeachment. When a Justice of the Supreme, Appellate or District Court is impeached then the Vice President of the CDA shall preside over the impeachment. The President or Vice President of the CDA shall not be convicted without the concurrence of two-thirds of all Members of Congress. A Supreme, Appellate or District Court Justice shall not be convicted without the concurrence of three-quarters of all Members of Congress and four-fifths of the President's Cabinet.

Judgment in cases of Impeachment shall not extend further than removal from Office, and disqualification to hold and enjoy any Office of honor, trust or government under the CDA. Regardless, the convicted person shall be liable and subject to indictment, trial, judgment and punishment according to law.

Section. 9. Election date, Congressional Sessions, Priority Session

All Federal and local elections shall be held on the second Tuesday of November. As needed and necessary, each public elementary, middle school or high school in a Congressional District will be made available to serve as a location for the act of voting by each qualified Citizen within the Congressional District. Each qualified Citizen shall be notified as to their location for voting at least two weeks ahead of election day by mail, email, phone or other convenient methods as specified by the qualified Citizen.

The Congress shall assemble by the later of January 3 or the first Tuesday of January of every year and be officially ended 16 days prior to the next Congress assembling. No one may abridge or amend the time period for Congress to convene. Each Member of Congress shall be given the month of July as vacation and 10 additional days, excluding Federal holidays and weekends, to be determined by each Member of Congress in consultation with the Member's party as to ensure that no more than five percent (5%) of the Members of Congress are on vacation at any given time other than in the month of July of each year or when Congress adjourns. Each Member of Congress shall be permitted to take the extra 10 days of vacation only from March 1 through October 31 or 5 days prior to Thanksgiving through 5 days after.

If the President of the CDA declares a Priority Session, and a simple majority of the Members of Congress concur through a public vote, then all vacations, meetings, travels and appointments outside of Washington DC will be cancelled and each Member of Congress will be obligated to stay in session until the matter which precipitated the President of the CDA to declare a Priority Session is fully resolved to the satisfaction of the President of the CDA and the majority of the Members of Congress. If Members of Congress do not agree and vote down the Priority Session, the President has the option to override the vote. However, if two-thirds of the Members of Congress vote to override the second call for a Priority Session by the President, the President may override Congress only with the consent of two-thirds of the Justices of the Supreme Court to convene the Priority Session. Otherwise, a Priority Session of Congress shall not be convened.

Section. 10. Election results to be certified by Congress; and rules, proceedings, journals and adjournment.

Congress shall certify all elections, returns and qualifications of its own Members, and a majority shall constitute a quorum to convene Congress and conduct Congressional business. However, one-third of the Members of Congress may compel the attendance of all of its Members. However, the ability of the minority of Members to recall all of the Members of Congress back into session does not in any way interfere with the majority of the Members of Congress to adjourn daily sessions at or beyond 6PM EST/EDT. Members of Congress shall outline penalties for unauthorized absences for its own Members.

Congress may determine the rules of its proceedings, punish its Members for disorderly behavior, unauthorized absences, and, with the concurrence of two-thirds of its Members, impeach a Member.

All Members of Congress must vote on all issues, no excuse shall be accepted other than verifiable hospitalizations in which the Member was involuntarily rendered unconscious, in a coma, or in mandatory surgery that was recommended and scheduled by the Member's doctor or doctors. Otherwise, the Member of Congress will be present in Congress to vote, make arrangements to vote remotely, or register a vote with the Leader of Congress and duly record and witness prior to the authorized absence. No abstentions will be allowed when voting on any issues subject to Congressional vote.

Congress shall keep a Journal of its proceedings, and from time to time publish the same, excepting such parts that may in their judgment, with the concurrence of the President, require secrecy due to national security; and the voting record of each Member of Congress on any question shall be entered in the Journal.

Once Congress is in session, Congress shall not adjourn for more than three days, including weekends, nor convene in any other place other than the Congressional building without the consent of the President of the CDA, unless in the case of a national emergency or war that threatens the physical well-being of the Members of Congress.

Section. 11. Legislative procedure.

All bills for raising revenue shall be approved by Congress.

Before becoming law, every bill which is approved by Congress shall be presented to the President for the President's approval: If the President approves, the President shall sign it, but if not, the President shall return it, with the President's objections to Congress, who shall enter the objections at large in the Congressional Journal, and proceed to reconsider it. If after such reconsideration two thirds of Congress agrees to pass the bill, the bill shall become law. Regardless, in all such cases the votes of each Member of Congress shall be determined by public vote, and the names of the Member voting for and against the bill shall be entered into the Journal. If any bill shall not be returned by the President within thirty-five (35) calendar days after it shall have been presented to the President, the same shall become law, as if the President had signed it, unless the Congress adjourns preventing the bill from returning, in which case it shall not become law.

All bills, appropriations, pending legislations, proposals, programs, budgets or the like that require the expenditure of money shall be considered one individual bill, item, appropriation, proposal, program, budget, spending requisition, and the like at a time and shall be voted on by Congress one individual bill, item, appropriation, proposal, program, budget, spending requisition, and the like at a time. Congress shall not package multiple bills, items, appropriations, proposals, programs, budgets, spending requisitions, and the like that spend money into one packaged bill, item, appropriation, proposal, program, budget, spending requisition, and the like for a single vote that would approve or disapprove two or more separate appropriations with one vote.

Members of Congress are forbidden to trade approval of one bill, pending legislation, order, resolution, or any matter requiring a vote in exchange for the approval of another and no deals for exchanging votes or backing of certain bills, pending legislation, order, resolution, or any matter requiring a vote shall be made between the Executive Branch of the government and Congress. Each bill, pending legislation, order, resolution, or any matter requiring a vote must stand on its own merits and each Member of Congress must review each bill accordingly.

Section. 12. Congressional control over budget and tax collections and other duties of Congress.

Congress shall have the power to assess and collect taxes, duties, imposts and excises, as prescribed in the Constitution to pay the debts and provide funding for only three broad Federal government responsibilities: 1) Self-defense; 2) Infrastructure, and 3) Education. All taxes, duties, imposts and excises shall be Just and, as much as possible, equally distributed among the People throughout the CDA;

The definitions of Self-defense, Infrastructure and Education will be interpreted in the narrowest possible manner according to the guidelines in this document and no creative definitions shall be given merit or consideration;

To borrow money on the credit of the Constitutional Democracy of America;

To regulate commerce within the CDA, with foreign nations, including the Indian Tribes;

To establish an uniform rule of naturalization, and uniform laws on the subject of bankruptcies throughout the CDA;

To coin money and fix the standard of weights and measures in the metric system;

To provide for the punishment of counterfeiting the securities and current coin of the CDA;

To establish Post Offices as and only as necessary;

To promote the progress of science and useful arts, by securing for limited times to authors and inventors the exclusive right to their respective creative works, discoveries, inventions and the like;

To constitute tribunals inferior to the Supreme Court;

To define and punish piracies and felonies committed on the high seas, the air or in space, and offences against the laws of nations;

To declare war and define the rules of engagement for our military;

To make rules for the government and regulation of the air, space, land and naval forces, including the army, navy, air force, marines and coast guard, and when and if necessary, a space force or some equivalent (together the Military);

To raise, fund and support the Military;

To provide for organizing, arming, and disciplining the Military, and for governing the conduct and behavior of the Military employed in the service of the CDA, to be codified in the Uniform Military Code of Conduct;

To provide for the calling forth of the Military to execute the laws of the CDA, suppress insurrections, repel invasions, and to engage in foreign conflicts to directly and indirectly protect the long-term welfare of the CDA;

Congress will also have the right to purchase, establish and exercise authority over all places purchased by the Federal government at fair market value, plus 10% for the construction of forts, magazines, arsenals, dock-yards, military bases, airports, research laboratories and facilities, and other buildings as necessary; and

To make all laws that are necessary and proper to carryout and execute the foregoing powers, and all other powers vested by this Constitution in the Federal government of the Constitutional Democracy of America, or in any Department, Agency, Bureau or Officer thereof.

Section 13. Congress shall make all laws, rules and regulations for territories governed by the CDA

The Congress shall have the power to dispose of and make all necessary laws, rules and regulations respecting the territory or other property belonging to the CDA; and nothing in this Constitution shall be so construed as to prejudice any claims of the CDA. Therefore, Congress shall make all laws, regulations, rules, and the like for all territories that are under the jurisdiction of the CDA with only consideration given to that which is Just.

Article VIII. Judicial Branch powers, duties, responsibilities.

Section. 1. Judicial power of the CDA will reside with the Supreme Court of the CDA.

The judicial Power of the CDA shall be vested in one Supreme Court and in such inferior courts as Congress may from time to time ordain and establish with the concurrence of the President. The judges, both of the Supreme and inferior courts, shall hold their offices for life as long as they are not convicted of a crime or treason and are mentally and physically capable of doing so, i.e., don't have dementia or Alzheimer's or the like and can communicate their thoughts in a clear and timely manner.

Section. 2. Judicial reach and authority.

The judicial power shall extend to all situations regarding matters of Justice arising under this Constitution, the laws of the CDA, and treaties negotiated by the President and ratified by Congress. In addition, all matters concerning cases involving admiralty, maritime, territorial, air and space jurisdiction, and involving controversies to which the CDA shall be a party and between residents of the CDA and foreign countries and their citizens, people or subjects.

In all cases affecting Ambassadors, other public Officials, General Consuls and Consuls, the Supreme Court shall have original jurisdiction. In all the other cases before mentioned, the Supreme Court shall have appellate jurisdiction, both as to law and fact.

The Supreme Court shall also render judgment as to the Just application under the Constitution of the EESP and NDRSP as presented to the Supreme Court by the President and Congress. The Supreme Court shall mediate and render all judgments to succession disputes for the Office of the President as outlined in this Constitution and the Chief Justice of the Supreme Court will preside over any Impeachment of any official of the CDA that would be subject to an Impeachment to affect the removal of the official from their official government position, except for a fellow Justice of the Supreme Court or a Justice of the Appellate or District Court. In the event that the President proposes the Impeachment of a Justice of the Supreme, Appellate or District Court, the majority of his Cabinet must support the proposal. If this should occur then the majority of the Members of Congress must also vote to Impeach the Supreme, Appellate or District Court Justice. If the majority of the Members of Congress vote to Impeach the Supreme, Appellate or District Court Justice then the Vice President shall preside over the Impeachment process and to effectuate the removal of the Supreme, Appellate, or District Court Justice from their position, three-quarters of Congress and four-fifths of the President's Cabinet, must also vote to remove the Supreme, Appellate or District Court Justice from their position. Congressional vote in this matter will be determined by a public vote that is publically broadcast, while the vote of the Cabinet Members will be conducted by secret ballot, but the result shall be publicly broadcast.

The trial of all crimes, except in cases of Impeachment, shall be tried by jury and such trial shall be held in the municipality where the said crimes shall have been committed; but when not committed within the territorial borders of the CDA, but where laws of the CDA prevail and where the CDA has jurisdiction over the lands, the trial shall be at such place or places as the Congress may by law have directed.

All first appeals will be directed to the District Courts (minimum of one per ten (10) Congressional District), the next appeal will be assigned to one of the existing 11 Federal Appellate Courts, and the last appeal will be assigned to the Supreme Court of the CDA for any criminal or civil judicial case.

Section. 3. Conviction and punishment for Treason.

Treason against the CDA shall be defined as waging open or covert war against the CDA or its People, conspiring to wage war against the CDA or its People with any foreign countries, organizations, institutions, entities, groups, or the like or domestic organizations, institutions, entities, groups, or the like, espionage against the CDA or divulging secrets of the CDA to persons, people, organizations, institutions, groups, entities or countries that are not authorized to have knowledge of the secrets of the CDA or giving aid and comfort to any enemies of the CDA, whether the enemy be an individual, organization, entity, group, institution, government, country or the like. No person shall be convicted of treason based solely on circumstantial evidence. For any individual to be convicted of treason, the testimony of at least two witnesses to the same act must be evidenced in open court, along with direct material evidence.

The Congress shall have power to declare the punishment for treason, but no descendants of the convicted traitor will bear the mark of their ancestors without proper trial and conviction. Also, the power of Congress to declare punishment for treason may include the forfeiture of wealth and assets, imprisonment or execution. However, in times of war, the penalty for treason must include execution.

Article IX. Federal government debt limits, Federal government budget and financial management.

Section 1. The Federal government must run a balanced budget

The Federal government must achieve a balanced budget at all times. However, should revenue expectations not meet budget or spending exceed budget, regardless of reason, Congress will be given one year to remedy deficits for all years. Should Congress not remedy the situation within one year, all Members of Congress will be under probation and given one additional year to remedy all deficits. Probation means that all Members of Congress their staff, aides and employees that directly work for Members of Congress will be under house arrest in their Washington, DC home and only allowed to and from Congress to work, no exceptions other than visits to doctors, dentists and hospital as absolutely and only necessary. In addition, all pay, and pension contributions will be suspended other than housing, transportation and food allowances, which shall be provided at the most basic and minimum levels necessary and deducted from pay. If after two years, Congress has not remedied all deficits, all Members of Congress their staff, aides and direct employees will be terminated from their positions, all pensions will be confiscated, all benefits will be terminated, and all pay that was withheld during the probation period shall be confiscated to pay down the deficit. Finally, all Members of Congress, their staff, aides and direct employees will be imprisoned for the same number of years that the person worked in Congress or as a staff, aide or direct employee of a Member of Congress. Immediately following the termination of the Members of Congress, the alternate Members of Congress will take office as prescribed in this Constitution. In anticipation of a deficit, Members of Congress, their aides, staff and direct employees shall not be allowed to resign, take a sabbatical or otherwise remove themselves from responsibility of creating the deficit. If the deficit materializes after the Member of Congress has left office, and it is deemed that the deficit resulted as a consequence of the previous Congress, the former Member of Congress will be subject to the same conditions as if the deficit occurred while the former Member of Congress was still in office. Therefore, the former Member of Congress will be allowed to participate in the process of deficit elimination, and on this matter alone, be allowed to vote.

Section 2. Repayment of Federal government debt.

As part of income tax collections, Congress will authorize the Internal Revenue Service (or its successor and assigns) to collect taxes for the repayment of Federal government debt. In addition, while the total Federal debt remains above allowed limits as outlined in this Constitution, Congress will create a plan to reduce the total Federal debt to allowed limits within fifty-one years immediately after the ratification of this document. The surcharge in income tax for the reduction of debt to allowed limits will be fairly borne by all the People of the CDA for the benefit of our future and future generations.

Section 3. Use of budget surplus.

Any budget surplus in any year will be used to pay down Federal government debt incurred to cover any outstanding budget deficits, first and foremost. Then, if there are no budget deficits outstanding since the ratification of this Constitution that needs to be remedied then all budget surpluses will be used to refund any Permitted Exceptional Spending (defined below) that was incurred. Next, any remaining Federal budget surpluses will be used to pay-down Federal government debt until Federal government debt is lowered to its allowable limits. Once the Federal government debt is reduced to allowable limits, any budget surplus will be accrued and set aside until the accrued amount plus any interest that it may have accrued equal the amount of allowed Federal government debt, plus 20% - this government account will be designated as the Principal Account. After the Principal Account is fully funded all excess budget surpluses will be set aside for three exceptional spending programs that meet all requirements outlined in this Constitution: 1) Natural Disaster Recovery Spending Plan (NDRSP; in case of natural disasters), 2) Emergency Economic Spending Plan (EESP; only due to economic recession or depression), or 3) for future war funding – the three referred together as the Contingency Funding. The total amount of Contingency Funding shall not exceed twice the total allowed Federal government debt. After Contingency Funding is fully funded, all budget surpluses will be refunded to the People of the CDA in following priority order until they receive a full refund: First, People that funded the repayment of Federal debt, second, People that funded the Principal Account, then finally People that funded the Contingency Funding. Any remaining balance shall be repaid to the People in a Just, but not necessarily equal, manner taking into consideration the amount of income taxes paid by any individual.

Section 4. Public debt not to be questioned; limit of national/Federal/CDA government debt; payment of debts.

The validity of the public debt of the CDA, authorized by law, including debts incurred for payment of Federal government elected officials and employees' salaries, compensation, benefits, pensions and rewards and the like in the course of their duties, obligations, work, and employment and the like, payment for the only three services the Federal government is permitted to engage on behalf of its People (largely, Self-Defense, Infrastructure and Education), and to pay interest and principal on the debt incurred by the Federal government shall not be questioned or denied.

Section 5. Limitation on the incurrence of debt by the Federal government.

The Federal government shall not incur debt of more than one-third of the average value of the most recent measurable 10-year period of the US gross domestic product.

Section 6. Contingency Funding procedure.

While the Federal government debt exceeds the allowable limits and the Principal Account is not 100% fully funded, Congress shall not be permitted to spend any money on anything else other than Self-Defense, Infrastructure and Education. Regardless, Congress may not spend any money on any social programs at any time – forever into the future – and are limited to spending money on Self Defense, Infrastructure, Education and one of three Permitted Exceptional Spending (PES; defined below).

PES must be deemed absolutely necessary by more than three-quarters of the Members of Congress and the President must approve such funding, then the Internal Revenue Service and Congress with input from the President and his staff, aides and direct reports will create a Contingency Funding plan, which must include the following: 1) How much money must be raised, 2) what it will be used for, 3) what objectives are expected to be achieved, 4) who stands to benefit from the PES, 5) how and from whom the money will be collected, and 6) how and to whom the money will be repaid over what period.

Permitted Exceptional Spending is limited to three items only: 1) NDRSP, 2) EESP, and 3) war funding. Once the President and Congress approve the Contingency Funding plan of the PES, it must then be immediately presented to the Supreme Court of the CDA and the Supreme Court of the CDA must determine with all due haste whether the plan is viable, and reasonably expected to achieve the objectives outlined, including who the benefits may accrue to, and whether the funding and repayment of the plan is viable and Constitutional, i.e., the People who fund the plan get their money back.

Any Members of Congress that opposed the Contingency Funding shall agree to select at least one advocate to argue against the approval of the Contingency Funding in front of the Supreme Court and this opposing advocate will be allowed to hire experts to prepare their case and any reasonable funding requirements for the development of the opposing case shall come from the Contingency Funding budget.

If the Supreme Court rejects the Contingency Funding plan, Congress, the President and the IRS will be permitted to present a revised plan two more times to the Supreme Court. If the Supreme Court rejects the two revised plans then no Contingency Funding will be permitted for the purposes outlined, until another Congressional vote is held and three quarters of the Members of Congress approve along with the President, a new Contingency Funding plan.

However, if the Federal government debt does not exceed the allowable limits, the Principal Account is 100% fully funded and at least some funding exists in the Contingent Funding Account then Congress shall be permitted to spend money to fund a PES to the limits of the monies in the Contingency Funding Account with the approval of the President. If the money in the Contingency Funding Account is depleted then Congress and the President must proceed as if the Federal government debt is above the allowed limits in order to spend monies on a PES. If a PES is fully authorized by Congress and the President and deemed as Just and Constitutional by the Supreme Court, the Internal Revenue Service will collect the funds for the PES through either a temporary surcharge in income taxes -- and separate and apart from normal income taxes -- or through a temporary national sales tax depending on the purpose taking into account beneficiaries, source of funding and the process of refunding the PES.

Section 7. Permitted Spending: Budgeting for Self- Defense, Infrastructure and Education.

The Federal government shall not collect income taxes for anything other than Self-Defense, Infrastructure and Education, together the Permitted Spending. In case of conflict in prioritizing spending, in general, priority shall be given to Self-Defense first then Education then Infrastructure. However, if an infrastructure project is deemed necessary or an emergency then priority will be given to the infrastructure spending first then Self-Defense then Education. However, in order to attain necessary or emergency status, an infrastructure spending project must garner the majority vote of Congress. However, no Member of Congress shall be permitted to vote, if the constituents of the

Member of Congress stand to benefit from the deemed necessary or emergency infrastructure project.

Definitions of the three items that encompass Permitted Spending follows:

1) Self-defense: Includes, but is not limited to the Military of the CDA, intelligence agencies such as the Central Intelligence Agency, Federal Bureau of Investigations, National Security Agency, Homeland Security, Secret Service and the like and its successors and assigns and the various executive branch departments such as Defense, State, Justice, and the like.

2) Infrastructure: Includes, but is not limited to roads, bridges, shipping and air ports, rail, courts, jails and prisons, information bureau, basic scientific research, space exploration, Federal Reserve Bank, banking/currency/financial systems, monitoring and enforcement departments, agencies, offices, commissions and bureaus such as the Securities and Exchange Commission, Environmental Protection Agency, Consumer Information and Protection Agency, Bureau of Land Management, Department of Parks and Forests, and the like and its successors and assigns, and the various executive branch departments such as Interior, Commerce, Treasury, and the like. However, no charities, social programs, subsidies, redistribution of wealth programs, special interest group spending and the like shall ever be part of the Federal infrastructure spending in any way, shape or form. And, when evaluating the necessity of any infrastructure program the substance of the program will be evaluated and not the form or superficial pretext of the potential infrastructure program. No programs shall exist or be supported by the Federal or local governments that take wealth or income from one group to provide for another in any way, shape or form. No redistribution of wealth shall ever be permitted in any way, shape or form.

3) Education: Pre-kindergartens, kindergartens, elementary schools, middle schools, high schools, colleges, universities, post-graduate programs, and doctorate and post-doctorate programs of the highest caliber and standards shall be maintained by the Federal government. In addition, the Federal government shall maintain, vocational schools at the high school equivalent level, specialized schools for developing skilled workers for all industries, including retraining programs for displaced workers, higher level specialized education programs such as medical schools, nursing schools, law schools, business schools, engineering and

science schools, and the like. Everyone who academically qualifies for any program shall be admitted on a need-blind basis.

Section 8. Repayment of subsidized government tuition.

If an individual benefits from Federal financial aid then the individual's income that is over one-quarter (25%) that of the average income of a Citizen over the last five-year period shall be subject to a minimum 10% surcharge tax to repay the Federal financial aid. This repayment plan will last until the individual has paid off all of the principal, plus an interest rate equivalent to the 30 year Federal bond rate plus an expected rate of inflation plus 3%. The term of this repayment plan shall be the lesser of 35 years or through five-years less than the person's expected retirement age.

Article X. Voting rights of Citizens.

Section 1. Voting limited to Citizens of the US 21 years and older

Participation in voting for Federal and local government offices shall be limited to Citizens of the CDA who are 21 years old and older who are mentally capable of understanding all of the issues necessary to determine their vote. In addition, no Citizens that are on probation under the criminal Justice system or incarcerated shall be allowed to vote.

Section 2. Right of certain Citizens to vote established.

The right of Citizens of the CDA 21 years old or older to vote in any election for government offices shall not be denied or abridged by the CDA or by any municipality on account of race, color, Philosophical beliefs, ancestry, creed, gender, sexual orientation, or based on any other potentially discriminating factor or category. The right of Citizens of the CDA to vote in any election for government office shall not be encumbered by any poll tax, fees or other encumbrances.

Article XI. Parity and Justice in law.

No laws shall be made by Congress that is not equally applied to all of the Citizens and legal Permanent Residents of the CDA, other than voting laws, and, where applicable, to Temporary Residents, foreign aliens or illegal residents other than where specifically prescribed under this document. No laws shall be made by Congress that favors one group of its Citizens and legal Permanent

Residents of the CDA over any other, and, where applicable, to Temporary Residents, foreign aliens or illegal residents other than where specifically prescribed under this document. Similarly, no laws shall be made by Congress that prejudices one group of its Citizens and legal Permanent Residents of the CDA over any other, and, where applicable, to Temporary Residents, foreign aliens or illegal residents other than where specifically prescribed under this document. Congress shall be permitted to make laws that apply only to Temporary Residents, foreign aliens or illegal residents in the CDA that govern immigration, residential-status issues, including the process to Citizenship, deportation, visas and, where applicable, diplomatic courtesies and rights.

Article XII. Separation of Philosophy and State.

Section 1. All Federal and municipal governments of the CDA will strictly observe the separation of Philosophy and state.

All governments in the CDA will strictly separate Philosophy and state in all respects, manner, function, ability, practice and way; no exception and no discretionary judgment will be permitted. This provision will be instituted with all haste without regard to cost and borne by the Citizens, legal Permanent Residents and Temporary Residents of the CDA through a one-time special tax.

Section 2. No references to any Philosophy shall be allowed.

No reference, mention, exhibit, indication, hint, visual aid, words, symbols or any other conveyance verbal, visual, auditory or feeling to any Philosophy, deity or the like shall be allowed in any oaths taken by any elected official – Federal or local – on currencies, in or on offices, venues, rooms, closets, floor, basement, roof, underground, above ground, on the ground, nook or cranny or the like on any Federal or local government buildings, or on any reports, filings, documents, recordings, visual materials, administrative aids or on any other object or visual, auditory, verbal or written communications, proclamations or declarations or the like.

Article XIII. The authorized collection of income taxes and revenue formation.

Section 1. Congress has the power to lay and collect income taxes.

The Congress shall have the sole power to lay and collect taxes on incomes as prescribed in this document and without regard to any census or enumeration for only the Permitted Spending, and, only when applicable, on Permitted Exceptional Spending.

Section 2. Specifically prohibited tax collections and exceptions.

No taxes shall be assessed on income from gambling, interest or dividends, no capital gains taxes shall be assessed, no inheritance tax or gift tax will be collected. No corporate income tax will be collected. Exception to this Section relates to investors whose primary source of income is in the form of interest, dividends or capital gains. For such individuals, their interest, dividend and capital gains shall be treated as ordinary income and taxed accordingly. Also, for those whose profession is deemed to be gambling, their income from gambling winnings shall also be subject to ordinary income taxes. However, those that have retired and whose primary source of income is interest, dividends or capital gains shall not be taxed on such sources of income. Abuse of the retirement exception shall result in confiscation of all assets up to the point of satisfying all back taxes owed plus an interest rate of 25% plus the rate on the 30 year Federal government bond plus rate of inflation.

Section 3. Teacher and professor pay.

Teacher and professor pay in Federal institutions: All full time teachers, professors, instructors and lecturers that have earned their bachelor's degree and are employees of the Federal education system will be paid at least 200% of the income of average Americans over the last five years, adjusted for cost of living in the area where they teach. Master's degree holders will earn at least 300% of the income of average Americans over the last five years, adjusted for cost of living in the area where they teach, while doctorate degree holders will earn at least 400% of the income of average Americans over the last five years, adjusted for cost of living in the area where they teach, and post-doctorate degree holders will earn at least 450% of the income of average Americans over the last five years, adjusted for cost of living in the area where they teach. All teachers, professors, instructors, and lecturers will be paid tax free.

Section 4. Scientific and basic research and funding for the scientific and basic research.

Those teachers and professors who conduct scientific, medical and basic research deemed necessary by industry, Congress and the President of the CDA, will be given a budget and time to conduct research in addition to their teaching obligations and will be given an additional stipend of 25% to 50% of their annual salary as compensation for their research efforts. Funds for research will be sourced from industries that are deemed to benefit from the research in aggregate – no exceptions – while funding for necessary research projects that have no immediate impact or benefit to specific industries will be collected through a Federal retail sales tax. Once specific benefits are realized by a particular industry or industries or by consumers in general, the Federal government will collect a surcharge from the industry or industries that benefit from the research or charge a national sales tax from consumers in general. In aggregate, revenue collected for scientific and basic research shall cover for all of the cost of scientific and basic research whether or not the scientific or basic research produced tangible benefits to industries or to the consumers. The recovery shall also provide for a 10%-20% additional surcharge, which shall be used to fund future scientific and basic research.

Section 5. Appropriations of money and reporting of accounting.

No money shall be drawn from the Treasury, but as a consequence of appropriations made by law; and a regular statement and account of the receipts and expenditures of all public money shall be published quarterly according to the same accounting rules that prevail over publicly traded companies in the CDA.

Section 6. Military pay shall not be taxed

Salaries and wages paid to Military personnel shall not be taxed in any way by any government entity in the CDA or by any other jurisdiction.

Article XIV. Terms, tenures, vacancies and protocols for succession.

Section 1. Terms of the President and Vice President.

The terms of the President and Vice President shall end at noon on the later of the third Tuesday of January or by the 20th day of January, but not on a Friday, Saturday or Sunday. The term of the next President and Vice President will begin immediately after the end of the term of the previous President and Vice President.

Section 2. Congress will convene once a year.

The Congress shall assemble at least once in every year, and such meeting shall begin at noon on the later of the first Tuesday of January or the third day of

January and continue through to sixteen (16) days prior to beginning of the next scheduled session of Congress.

Section 3. Filling the vacancy in the Office of the President.

At the time set for the beginning of the term of the President, if the President-elect shall have died then the Vice President-elect shall become President. If a President shall not have been chosen before the time set for the beginning of the new President's term due to a necessary recounting of the vote then the previous President shall continue as President until the recount is completed or all of the candidates concede the election to a single candidate. This recounting shall not take place for more than three months past the date of election. If a President shall not have been chosen before the time set for the beginning of the new President's term due to an unforeseen result then the previous President shall continue as President until an election is arranged. This election must take place no more than six months past the official date for electing a President. If the President-elect is disqualified from becoming President then the Vice President elect shall become President. If the Vice President elect is also disqualified then the Speaker of the Congress shall assume the position of President until a new election for President can be arranged, which must take place no later than six (6) months after when the Speaker of the Congress assumes the post of President. In time of war, elections will continue as normal unless the territories of the CDA have been invaded by a foreign nation or power. If the territories of the CDA have been invaded by a foreign nation or power, elections will continue as normal as long as more than three-quarters of the territories of the CDA as measured by population are still under the control and influence of the CDA and protected by its Military. If more than a quarter of the territories of the CDA, as measured by population, is occupied and controlled by a foreign power then the previous President of the CDA will continue as President until conditions for elections are met, at which point the election for President will be held six months after the permissible conditions for election are met.

Section 4. Vacancy in office of Vice President.

Whenever there is a vacancy in the office of the Vice President, the President shall nominate a Vice President who shall take office upon confirmation by a majority vote of Congress.

Section 5. No other means of transfer of power shall be recognized.

All transfer of power in the Constitutional Democracy of America shall be achieved through direct election of President, Vice-President and Members of Congress. All other forms of transfer of power shall not be recognized, acknowledged or endorsed by the People, including violent revolutions or insurrections, coup d'états, public or otherwise, brokered transfer of powers, through secret deals or other means that are invisible or murky to the People of the CDA. Also, no foreign powers will have any influence, oversight, input, a hand in, or aiding the transfer of power in the CDA in any way, shape or form at any level of government.

Section 6. No individual shall participate in the transfer of power other than through direct elections.

Anyone participating in any other means to transfer power in the CDA other than through legal campaigning and direct elections will be deemed a traitor and shall be confined to prison for the rest of their natural life.

Section 7. Violation of campaign promises will be a criminal offense.

Anyone making campaign promises will be held to the standards of a court room testimony. Therefore, anyone breaking any campaign promises, whether at the Federal or local level, will be held in contempt of the People and will be dismissed from office and fined the total of the compensation received while the official held government office and will be subject to a minimum of 10 years in prison.

Section 8. Power of Congress in Presidential succession.

Congress will have the sole right to determine the succession line for the President of the CDA beyond what has been prescribed in this document should both the President and Vice President die or could not continue in their capacity as President and Vice President. Members of Congress will not only determine the line of succession beyond what has been prescribed in this document, but also replace with all haste those Members of Congress that would be in line of succession for President should such Members be incapacitated, dead or otherwise unable to execute their duties.

Article XV. Presidential terms, governance, and succession.

Section 1. Term of the President and limit to number of terms a President may serve.

Each term of the President shall be for five years. No person shall be elected to the office of the President more than twice, and no person who has held the office of President, or acted as President, for more than two years and six months of a term to which some other person was elected President shall be elected to the office of the President more than once.

Section 2. Vice President as Acting President.

Whenever the President transmits to the Speaker of Congress, the Majority Leader of Congress, the Minority Leader of Congress and the Supreme Court the President's written declaration that the President is unable to discharge the powers and duties of the office, and until the President transmits to them a written declaration to the contrary, such powers and duties of the President shall be discharged by the Vice President as Acting President.

Section 3. Vice President as Acting President when the President is incapacitated.

Whenever the majority of either the principal officers of the Executive Departments or the majority of the Members of Congress transmit to the Speaker of Congress, the Majority Leader of Congress, the Minority Leader of Congress and to the Supreme Court their written declaration that the President is unable to discharge the powers and duties of the Office of President, the Vice President shall immediately assume the powers and duties of the Office as Acting President.

Thereafter, when the President transmits to the Speaker of Congress, the Majority Leader of Congress, the Minority Leader of Congress and the Supreme Court, the President's written declaration that no incapacity exists, the President shall resume the powers and duties of the Office of President unless the Vice President and a majority of either the principal officers of the Executive Department or the majority of the Members of Congress transmit within four days to the Speaker of Congress, the Majority Leader of Congress, the Minority Leader of Congress and the Supreme Court their written declaration that the President is unable to discharge the powers and duties of his office. Thereupon, the Supreme Court and Congress shall decide the issue, assembling within forty-eight hours for that purpose if not in session. The Chief Justice of the Supreme Court will act as the mediator and arbiter of the issue while the Congress debates the issue with the advice of the Supreme Court Justices. Once convened for the determination of the competency of the President, Congress will have 21 days to determine whether or not the President is competent to continue to discharge the powers and duties of the President of the CDA. If Members of Congress determine by two-thirds majority vote and the Supreme Court agrees that the vote was Constitutional, also by two-thirds majority vote, and all procedures were followed as outlined in the Constitution that the President is not competent to discharge the powers and duties of the President then the Vice President shall continue to discharge the same as Acting President; otherwise, the President shall resume the powers and duties of the office of President.

Article XVI. Commerce clauses.

Section 1. No import/export duties.

No tax or duty shall be laid on articles exported from the CDA nor imported to the CDA unless in retaliation for unjust taxes levied on CDA goods and services exported to foreign countries by foreign entities.

Section 2. No preference for ports of entry

No preference shall be given by any regulation of commerce or revenue to the ports of entry of one location over those of another; nor shall any forms of transportation bound to, or from, one port of entry, be obliged to enter, clear, or pay duties in another.

Article XVII. No title of nobility and no foreign office holdings.

Section 1. No nobles or royals in the CDA.

No title of nobility or royalty shall be granted by the CDA and no Citizen of the CDA shall accept titles of nobility or royalty without the prior consent of the President and the majority consent of Congress of the CDA. Any person who was a noble or royal at the time of naturalization to a Permanent Resident of the CDA shall be permitted to retain their title, but it shall not be inured or passed-down to future generations, if future generations would want to remain a Citizen or Permanent Resident of the CDA. Temporary Residents will be allowed to retain titles of nobility or royalty and be permitted to inure or pass-down such title to their children as permitted by the laws of the foreign country that granted the title, assuming the foreign entity continues to recognize the title.

No person holding any official government post shall, without the consent of the President and majority consent of Congress, accept any present, emolument, office, honor or title of any kind, from any foreign head of state, foreign country, foreign organization, foreign legislature or foreign judicial institution.

Article. XVIII. Congress shall have the power to amend the Constitution.

The Congress shall have the sole power to amend this Constitution should two-thirds of Congress and the President of the CDA approve the proposed amendment. However, the Congress shall make no laws, rules, regulations, legislation or the like to limit, restrict, curb, suspend, countermand or revoke any Inalienable Rights provided in this Constitution under Article II to the People of the CDA. Congress shall not make any laws, rules, regulations, legislation or the like to provide for social programs, charities, subsidies, redistribution of wealth, progressive taxes, tax shelters, loop holes, deductions, corporate taxes, incentives, or other similar government funded programs.

Article. XIX. The Constitution, and all laws stemming from the Constitution, shall be obeyed, and all government officials shall take a non-Philosophical oath or affirmation to support the Constitution.

This Constitution, and the laws of the CDA which shall be made in pursuance thereof; and all treaties made, or which shall be made, under the authority of the CDA, shall be the supreme law of the land; and all residents of the CDA, including judges, shall be bound thereby, anything in the Constitution or laws to the contrary notwithstanding.

All government officials, including the President, Vice President, Executive Department heads, Members of Congress, Judges, members of the Military, and all other Federal and local government personnel shall be bound by a non-Philosophical oath of affirmation to support this Constitution; and no Philosophical test shall ever be required as a qualification to any office or public trust under the CDA.

Article. XX. Effectuation of the Constitution.

To take effect and become the law of the land, this Constitution must be approved by two-thirds of both Houses of Congress of the USA, two-thirds of the states of the USA, and approved by the President of the USA.

www.ingramcontent.com/pod-product-compliance
Lightning Source LLC
Chambersburg PA
CBHW072211270326
41930CB00011B/2613

* 9 7 8 0 6 1 5 8 1 8 1 8 4 *